Stephen Westland
and Maggie Maggio

The Pocket

Universal Principles of Color

100 Key Concepts

for Understanding, Analyzing, and Working with Color

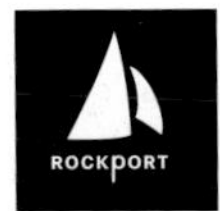

CONTENTS / ALPHABETICAL

CONTENTS / PATHWAYS

INTRODUCTION

How different our lives would be without the gorgeous reds and yellows of a sunset, the blinding blues and yellows of a beach holiday, and the effervescent greens of a rain forest. Color is vital to our emotional well-being. Yet, in art and design it also imparts meaning, conveys information, contributes to aesthetics, and induces affective responses in the viewers of artwork.

Color is not an integral, visible part of objects. Rather, it is the brain's response to light reflected by objects. Isaac Newton understood this more than 300 years ago when he wrote that "the rays are not coloured." Despite the advances made in the science of color since then, we cannot understand how colors work together without considering the contribution of artists. As Paul Cézanne put it, "Color is the place where our brain and the universe meet." During much of the twentieth century, Newton's and Cézanne's words were overlooked; the teaching of color focused on ideological principles that confuse rather than illuminate. But now, groundbreaking advances in science and technology are reconnecting us to color and light.

The Pocket Universal Principles of Color presents one hundred topics that are critical to understanding the effective use of color. The authors blend ideas from art, philosophy, design, biology, physics, chemistry, and cognitive science to provide an essential foundation for putting the science and art of color to work.

PATHWAYS

We have designed this book to be used in two ways—hence, the two different tables of contents. The first lists, in standard alphabetical order, individual color principles. Each one is self-contained, though we provide references to other related entries. The second consists of distinct pathways based on nine topics of color study ranging from science and industry to art and design. Each pathway provides a sequence of entries color-coded by topic area. We suggest reading entries in each topic area in the order given in our Content/Pathways page. We think of this as a color itinerary, with road maps that you can follow on your color journey.

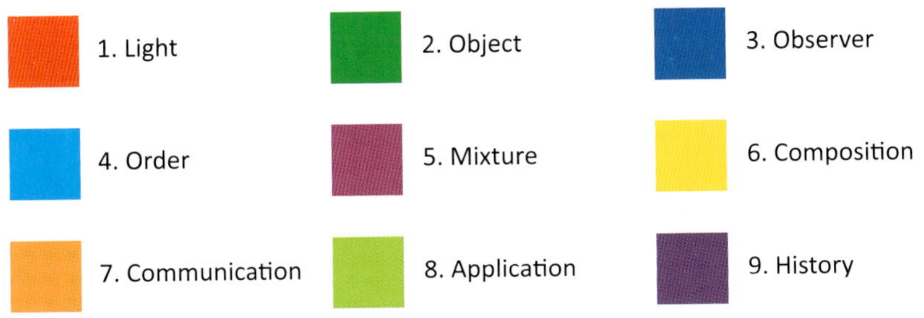

1. Light 2. Object 3. Observer

4. Order 5. Mixture 6. Composition

7. Communication 8. Application 9. History

01 #THEDRESS

A 2015 internet meme in which people saw a digital photo of a two-color dress as either blue and black or white and gold

- The digital photo became an internet sensation because the dress appeared to have different colors at different times. Some people saw it as blue and black; others as white and gold. Posted on BuzzFeed, the image attracted more than 10 million tweets within a week.

- There is no consensus on what aspect of human color vision caused this phenomenon, but the fact that the image was closely cropped and overexposed was a likely factor.

- The fact that the dress appeared to be different colors to different people, and even to the same person at different times, proved that color is a perception rather than a fixed property of an object.

- The furor prompted vision scientists and neurologists to ask new questions about our perception of color and its constancy.

#TheDress is a reminder that the context in which a color appears in a design can have a profound effect on its appearance.

SEE ALSO Color Constancy • Human Visual System • Perception Triangle

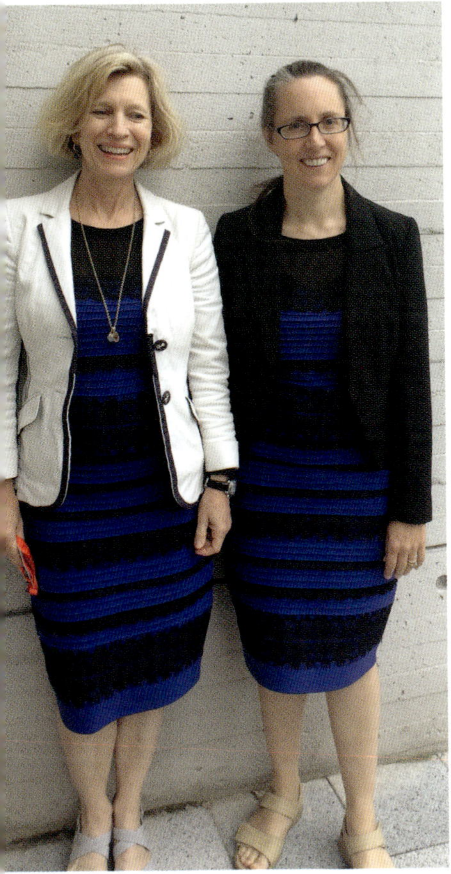

Professor of Visual Neuroscience Anya Hurlbert and Professor of Vision Science Jenny Read, Newcastle University (left to right), at the European Conference on Visual Perception (ECVP), 2015, Liverpool, UK. It was the digital image of the dress (which was overexposed) rather than the dress itself that caused people to see different colors.

BuzzFeed posted the photo with a poll: Is it white and gold or blue and black? The poll triggered millions of responses, with 2.5 million votes for white and gold and 1.2 million for blue and black. The actual dress was blue and black.

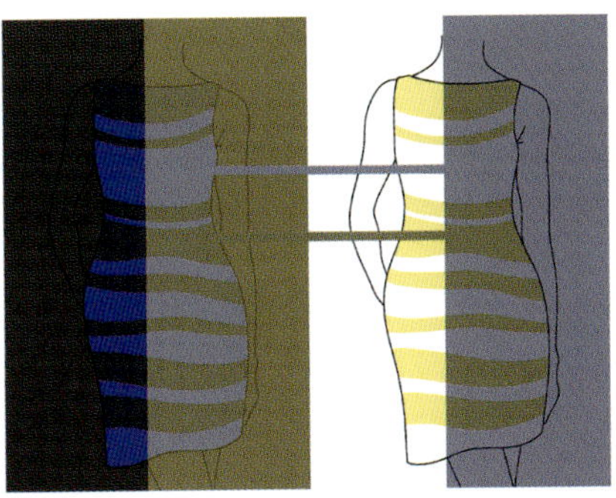

Individuals' interpretation of the colors of the dress depended on their assumptions about the lighting conditions.

02 ACCESSIBILITY

Design color combinations with enough contrast to make the content clearly legible for people with limited vision

- Vision impairment includes low vision, which cannot be corrected by glasses, contacts, or surgery, as well as age-related conditions such as glaucoma, cataracts, and diabetes.

- Roughly 1 in 12 males and 1 in 200 females have so-called color blindness. They can, in fact, see color, but those with the most common types of the condition cannot distinguish between red and green.

- Web design accessibility is assessed by the Web Content Accessibility Guidelines (WCAG). The latest version awards three accessibility-level standards (AAA, AA, and A).

It is important to consider accessibility at the design stage and avoid situations where text and background are similar in lightness.

SEE ALSO Contrast • Lightness • Limited Color Vision • Trichromacy

RULE OF TINCTURE

"Metals shall not be put on metals, nor colors on colors."

The medieval rule of tincture is based on the fact that most of the vivid hues have a mid to low lightness and do not contrast with black, while vivid yellows have a high lightness and do not contrast with white. This rule was first used in heraldry to ensure the legibility of the design on a coat of arms, but it remains a useful guide in graphic design.

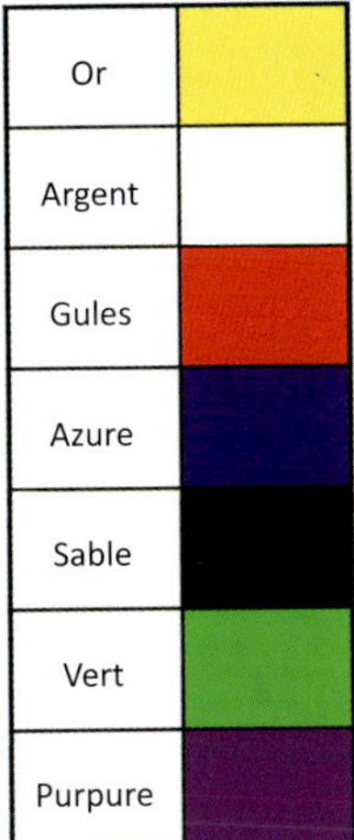

METALS: The first is Or (gold/yellow); the second is Argent (silver/white).

COLORS: The third is Gules (red); fourth, Azure (blue); fifth, Sable (black); sixth, Vert (green); and seventh, Purpure (purple).

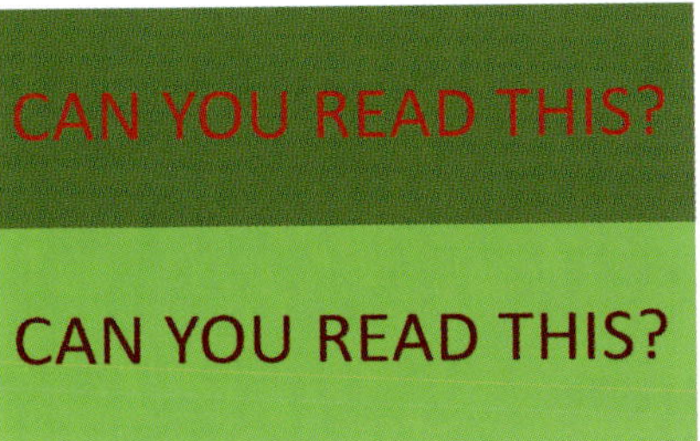

Red on green? Although there is hue contrast in this image, the top text example "Can You Read This?" does not follow the rule of tincture. One solution is to lighten the background and darken the text. This makes the text more accessible.

03 ADDITIVE MIXTURE

The process and effect of combining colored lights

- Additive mixture describes the process by which different lights appear to be combined and the colors that result from this process. The lights are not mixed per se, but spatially coincident or so close together that they cannot be resolved by the eye.

- This creation of new colors is a property of the human visual system, which records the response of light-sensitive cells in the retina called cones.

- The optimal set of additive primaries that results in the largest color gamut in light are red, green, and blue (RGB). For that reason, this is the default color space for working with digital designs. Although it can generate all hues, it cannot generate all variations of the colors that we can see.

- Display manufacturers often use slightly different red, green, and blue primaries in their systems. Nevertheless, the three-primary principle of additive color mixture has allowed the development of color imaging technologies such as television, cameras, projection systems, and emissive displays.

SEE ALSO CMYK • RGB • Subtractive Mixture

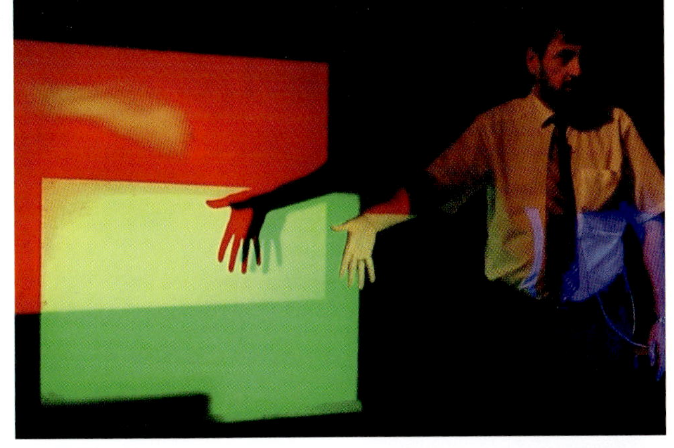

Projected light: additive mixture of projected lights (red + green = yellow). The overlapping of projected lights is an example of additive mixture. In this case, the additive mixture of red and green produces yellow.

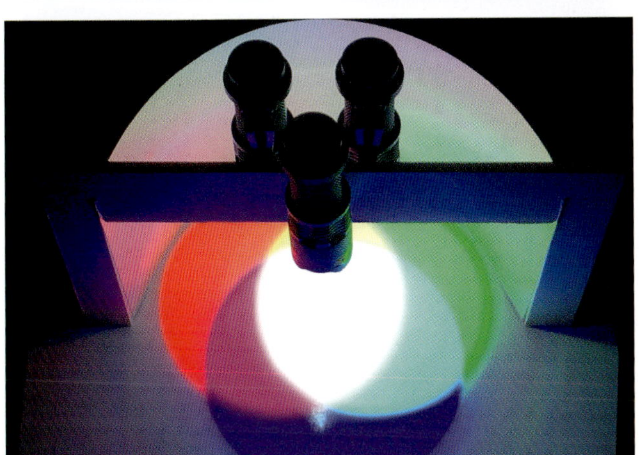

The overlapping of RGB LED flashlights produces the additive mixture of white.

04 ADVANCING AND RECEDING

Colors can appear to be in front of or behind one another, creating the illusion of depth in two dimensions

- It is often said that warm colors advance and cool colors recede. While it may be true that a vivid red swatch will appear to be closer than the same-sized vivid blue swatch, this is not a factor of hue but of chroma.

- Vivid blues are lower in chroma than vivid reds. The reverse effect of blue advancing and red receding is possible if the chromatic relationship is shifted, as illustrated by the four squares (opposite).

In intentionally manipulating color to create a sense of depth, attention must be paid to the relative lightness and chroma as well as the relationship of figure and ground.

SEE ALSO Atmospheric Perspective • Chroma • Warm and Cool

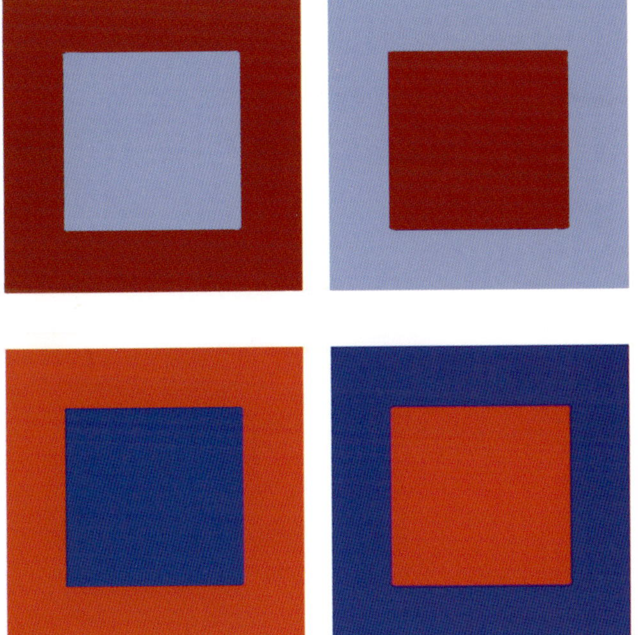

Compare the figure-ground relationships of the four variations on the left. Do the smaller squares appear to be on top of the larger squares or behind the frame created by the larger squares?

05 ALBERS'S *INTERACTION OF COLOR*

The seminal text on color in context by Josef Albers published in 1961

- Trained as an art teacher, Josef Albers was a student and then a teacher at the Bauhaus in the 1920s and early 1930s. His teaching methods included "... construction experiments with straw, matchboxes, paper and wire."

- When the Bauhaus closed in 1933, Albers taught at Black Mountain College in North Carolina, where his course focused on color phenomena with paper as his medium. Starting in 1950, as director of the Department of Design at Yale, he taught drawing and color courses with a perception-based approach that influenced generations of artists, designers, and teachers.

- In *Interaction of Color* Albers wrote, "In visual perception a color is almost never seen as it really is—as it physically is. This fact makes color the most relative medium in art. To use color effectively it is necessary to recognize that color deceives continually."

Although the notion that color is physical is contentious today, the key idea that color perception is relative has stood the test of time.

SEE ALSO Simultaneous Contrast • Warm and Cool

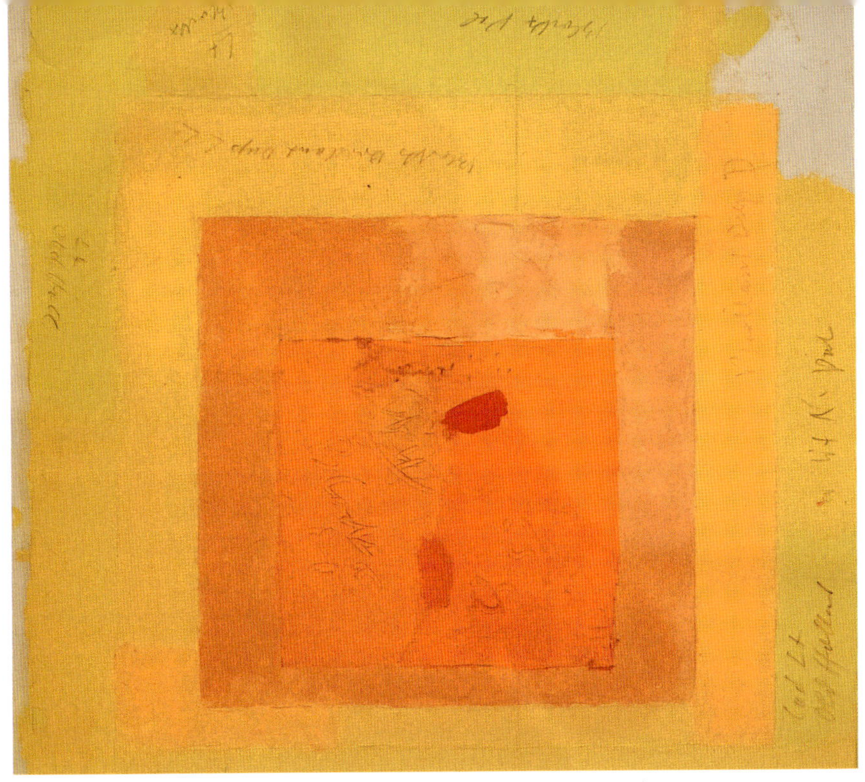

Color study for *Homage to the Square,* by Josef Albers. In his world-famous series, *Homage to the Square,* Albers explored the relationship of colors in more than 1,000 paintings between 1950 and his death in 1976.

ATMOSPHERIC PERSPECTIVE

Also called aerial perspective; the technique of representing more-distant objects as being less distinct, bluer, and more muted

- In *A Treatise on Painting*, Leonardo da Vinci wrote that in nature, "Colors become weaker in proportion to the distance from the person looking at them."

- Artists and designers can create an illusion of depth by softening edges, limiting detail, and reducing the lightness contrast between distant objects.

- In the "Blue" chapter of *The World According to Color*, James Fox wrote, "Horizons are often blue because of ... aerial perspective: as objects recede from us, they are veiled by ever more scattered light, appearing progressively bluer, before terminating in a hazy cerulean horizon."

In summary, objects in the distance appear to become progressively smaller in size, less detailed, weaker in chroma, faded and lighter, and bluer depending on the time of day.

SEE ALSO Chroma • Rayleigh Scattering

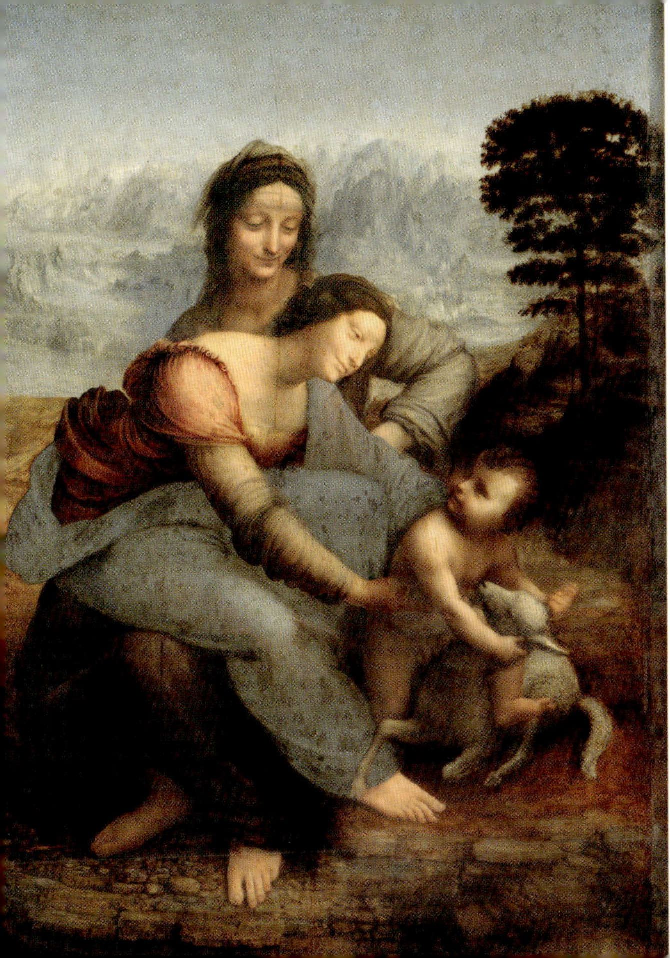

The Virgin and Child with Saint Anne (1510), by Leonardo da Vinci. The mountains fading into the distance are an example of atmospheric perspective.

07 BALANCE

The subjective perception of unity combining proportion and the visual weight of colors

- Balance is a key element of design, but what feels balanced to one person may feel unsettling to another.

- Traditional guidelines for developing a color scheme include using set proportions of complementary colors, and selecting dominant, supporting, and accent colors.

- Usually, illustrations using traditional guidelines show only vivid hues. But hue is only part of the equation. Variations in lightness and chroma, such as pale, muted, and dark versions of the hue, each have different visual weights that affect the overall balance.

It is more effective to balance color by considering not only the hue contrasts but also the relative proportions of lightness and chroma.

SEE ALSO Color Schemes • Complementary Colors

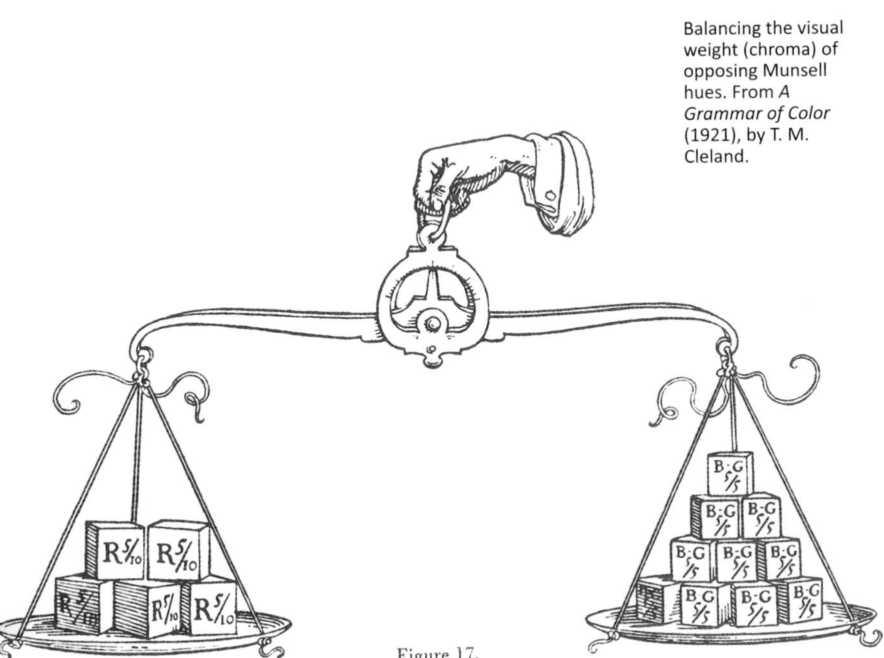

Balancing the visual weight (chroma) of opposing Munsell hues. From *A Grammar of Color* (1921), by T. M. Cleland.

Figure 17.

BASIC COLOR TERMS

Eleven basic color terms—white, black, red, yellow, green, blue, brown, pink, purple, orange, and gray—are widely understood regardless of culture and language

- The notion of eleven basic color terms developed from a 1969 study by Brent Berlin and Paul Kay.

- The study spurred a debate between Universalists who, like Berlin and Kay, believe that color perception is the same for everyone, and Relativists, who argue that color perception is influenced by our culture and language.

- More recent studies indicate that, while there are likely universal constraints on color naming, differences in language may affect color perception to some extent.

Beyond the basic color terms, language becomes much less precise. It is necessary to learn additional terms to describe lightness and chroma accurately.

SEE ALSO Character Zones • Munsell System • Three Dimensions of Color

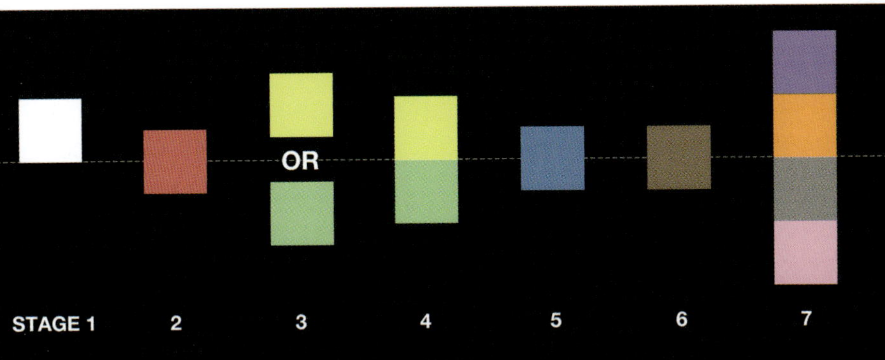

The seven stages of language development for color terms according to the Berlin and Kay study: black and white (stage 1); red (stage 2); yellow or green (stage 3); yellow and green (stage 4); blue (stage 5); brown (stage 6); and purple, orange, gray, and pink (stage 7). There is ongoing controversy about how many basic color terms there are and whether these apply to all cultures and languages.

09 BAUHAUS

German art and design school that made seminal contributions to twentieth century architecture, design, and color education

- The Bauhaus was founded in Germany in 1919 by architect Walter Gropius. Its program influenced modern color theory and practice.

- Bauhaus-trained artists Johannes Itten, Josef Albers, Wassily Kandinsky, and Paul Klee made notable contributions to color theory.

- Itten was known for his studies of color contrasts; Albers focused on the relativity of color.

- When the Bauhaus closed in 1933, Gropius and many faculty members, including Albers and architect Ludwig Mies van der Rohe, emigrated to the United States.

SEE ALSO Albers's *Interaction of Color* • Itten's *The Art of Color*

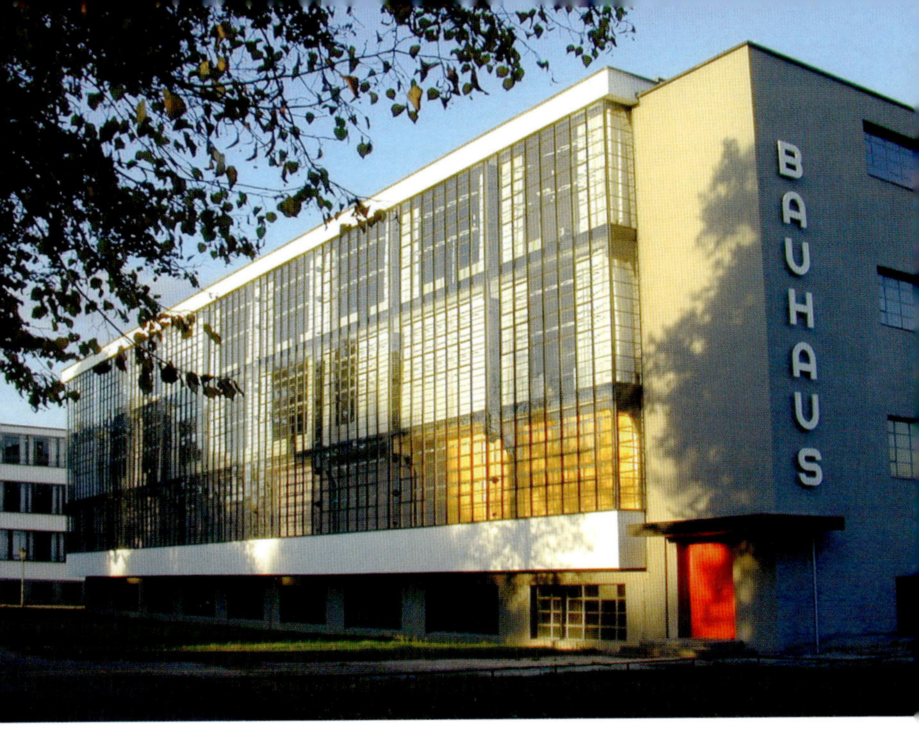

The Bauhaus operated in three German cities. This building in Dessau, designed by Bauhaus founder Walter Gropius, was the most iconic location.

10 BEZOLD EFFECT

The substitution of a single color causes every other color in the design to shift in relationship

- The Bezold Effect is named after the German professor Wilhelm von Bezold (1837–1907), who observed in the nineteenth century that a color may appear different depending on its relation to adjacent colors. The Bezold Effect refers to the phenomenon where changing a single color in a design causes the perceptual color of every other color in the design to shift. The apparent changes to the other colors in the design are not always consistent; for example, some colors in the pattern may become darker and others lighter.

- One version of the Bezold Effect is shown opposite. It is an example of how just changing the outline color of a pattern can dramatically alter its appearance.

Understanding that form affects color and color affects form is of particular significance in 2D design, such as textiles and wallpaper.

SEE ALSO Partitive Mixture • Simultaneous Contrast

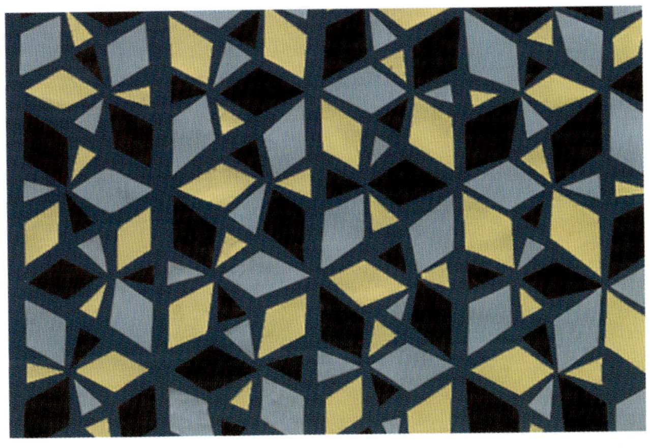

Outline effect: Changing the color of the outline in the pattern affects the overall perception of the color scheme.

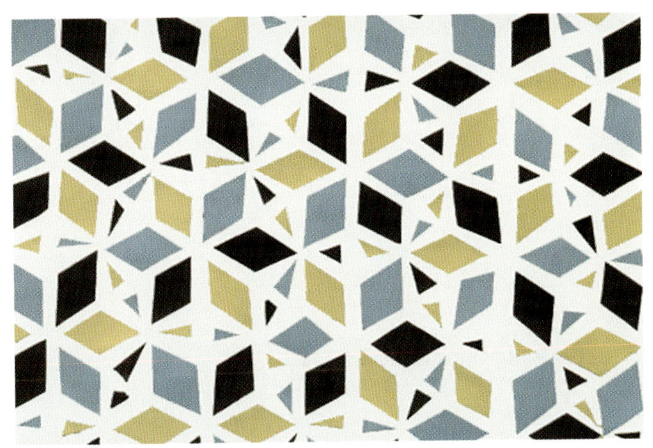

11 BLACK AND WHITE

The darkest and lightest of the colors

- Value studies in black and white are often the first step in creating a work of art or design because they are the quickest way to evaluate the lightness contrasts.

- Black and white are achromatic colors, having neither chroma nor hue. The gray colors between them often have undertones of hue; in this case they are called chromatic grays.

- The blackest paint available so far is Musou Black with a light absorption rate of 99.4%. A nanomaterial coating called Vantablack®, developed by Surrey NanoSystems, absorbs 99.965% of light.

- At the opposite end of the spectrum, scientists at Purdue University have developed an ultra-white paint that reflects more than 98% of light.

SEE ALSO Colorants • Grisaille

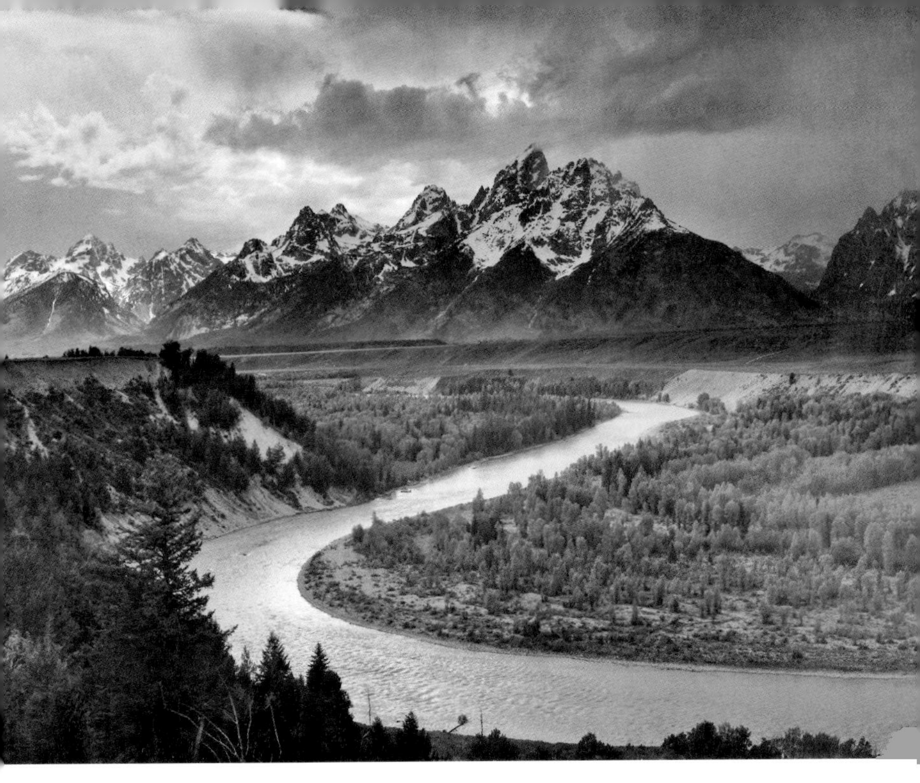

The Tetons and the Snake River (1942), a photograph by Ansel Adams. Adams's Zone System achieved the desired final print through understanding how the tonal range of an image depends on exposure, development, and printing in photography.

12 BLUE LIGHT

The intensity and color of light can interfere with natural sleeping patterns and overall well-being

- A 2013 report showed that blue lights installed on Tokyo's subway platforms reduced suicides by 84%, sparking interest in both the beneficial and harmful effects of color and light.

- Our visual system contains five photopigments: Three mediate color vision. One controls night vision. The fifth, melanopsin, helps regulate the circadian system.

- It is now established that a consistent pattern of light and dark is essential for good health. Exposure to too much light just before sleeping and/or insufficient light in the hours after waking can negatively impact sleep and overall well-being.

Our increasing understanding of the effect of light on health and well-being is impacting how lighting is being used in the design of our homes and workplaces.

SEE ALSO Human Visual System • Lighting

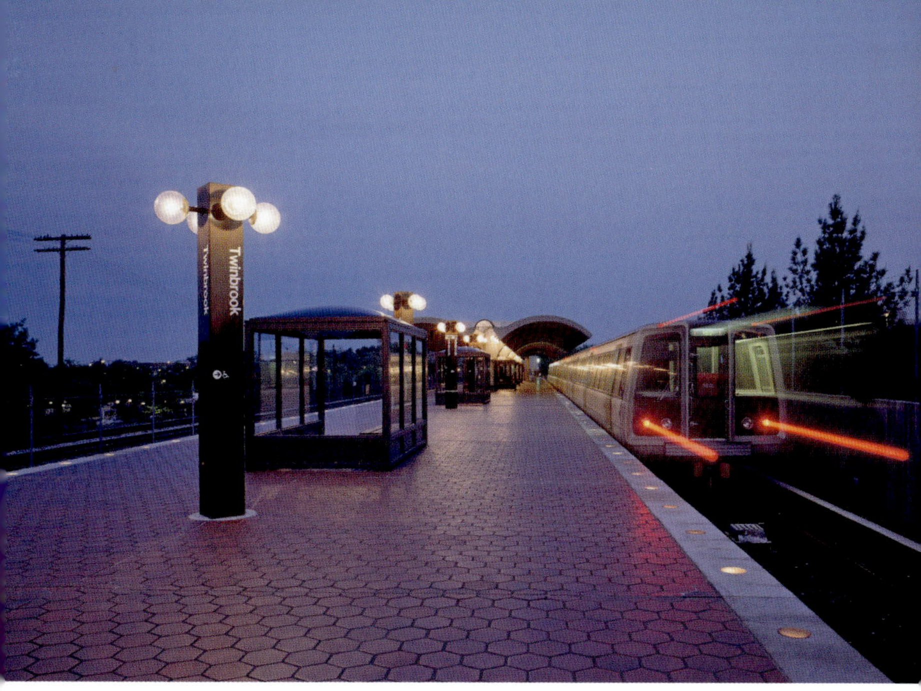

Installation of blue light at subway stations in Tokyo has led to various installations of light systems in several locations globally with claims about effects on human health and performance. Whether these effects are genuine is still being researched.

13 BRAND COLORS

A small set of specific colors that are strongly linked with a company, a product, or an institution

- In many cases, the color of a product or its packaging is vital for success. It is best achieved using colors that communicate ideas and emotions that are consistent with the brand's values.

- Coca-Cola's famous use of red for branding began in its earliest years, when its barrels were painted red so they could be easily distinguished from alcohol barrels.

- In many countries, it is possible to protect the use of specific brand colors through a trademark.

Color is a vital component of the visual identity of brands and can aid brand recognition and recall.

SEE ALSO Color Forecasting • Color Meaning • Symbolic Color

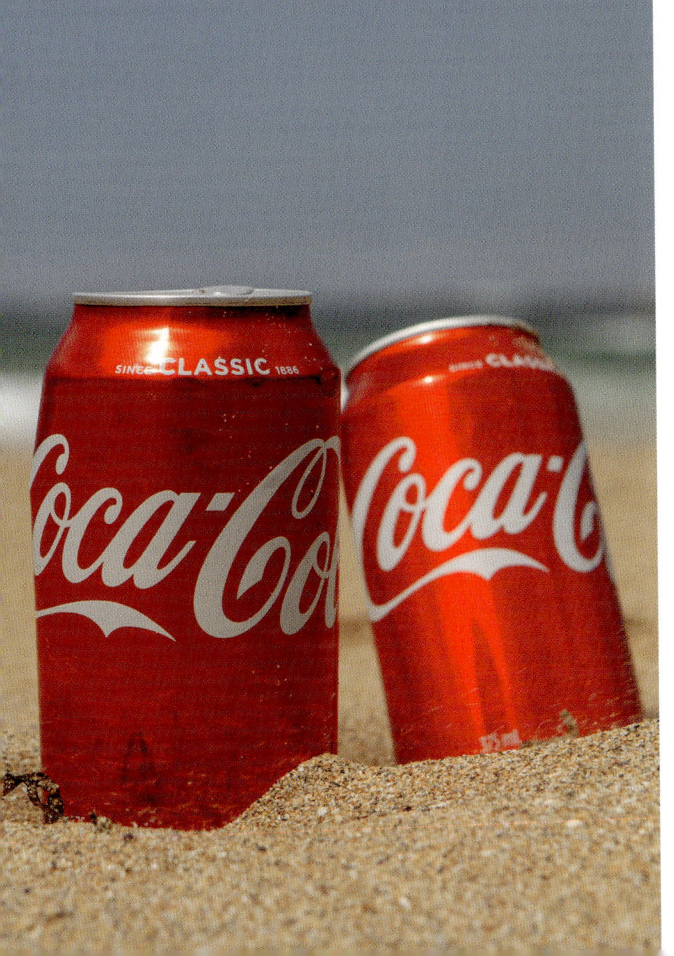

The use of red and white in the classic Coca-Cola can is firmly established by the market leader and is a generic color code in this product category.

14 CAMOUFLAGE

Pattern designs inspired by animals in nature who often avoid detection by blending with their surroundings

- The use of camouflage for military applications became widespread during World War I. France is believed to be the first country to create a dedicated camouflage unit in 1915. (In French, the word *camouflage* means "to make up for the stage.") Originally used on guns and vehicles, camouflage is now ubiquitous in military clothing.

- The potential for use of camouflage in fashion was picked up by *Vogue* in 1943 and became mainstream when Andy Warhol produced a series of camouflage prints in the 1980s. Popular through the 1990s and the early 2000s, the camo trend in fashion is once again on an upswing.

Camouflage is just one example of how artists and designers can be inspired by what they observe in nature.

SEE ALSO Chemistry of Chromophores

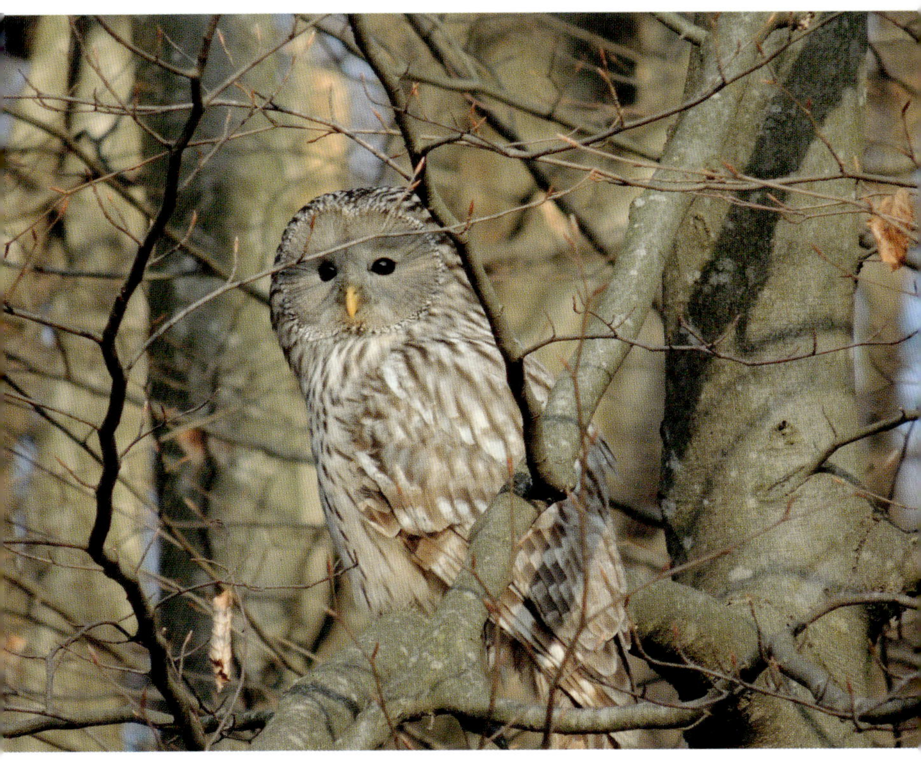

An owl blending into the background is a classic
example of natural camouflage.

15 CHARACTER ZONES

The parts of a color space that share perceptual similarities independent of hue

- The basic character zones are vivid, pale, muted, and dark. Pale colors are noticeably lighter than the most vivid version of the same hue. Muted colors appear grayer, and colors in the dark zone look darker. Achromatic colors are in the neutral zone.

- In Japan, the Practical Color Coordinate System and the Hue and Tone System use the English word *tone* for the combination of value and chroma, with colors of the same tone falling into the same character zone.

- In some color order systems, the character zone is not identified. In Munsell, a color's position is determined by value and chroma; in RAL. by lightness and chroma. In the Natural Color System (NCS), nuance refers to the combination of blackness and chromaticness, which, together with hue, locates a color in a specific zone.

In designing a color scheme, it is often the dominant character zone, rather than the hue, that communicates the most meaning.

SEE ALSO Color Meaning • Munsell System • Natural Color System • Tint, Shade, and Tone

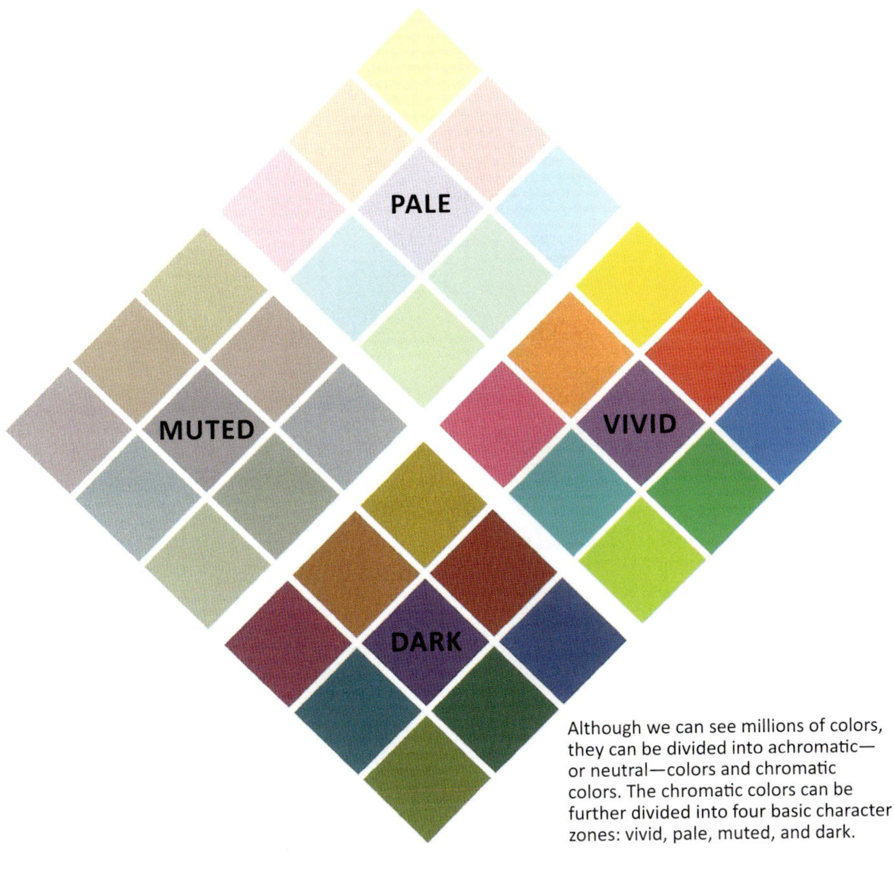

Although we can see millions of colors, they can be divided into achromatic—or neutral—colors and chromatic colors. The chromatic colors can be further divided into four basic character zones: vivid, pale, muted, and dark.

16 CHEMISTRY OF CHROMOPHORES

The chromophore is the part of a molecule responsible for its color

- The absorption of light by dyes and pigments is due primarily to electronic transitions enabled by the molecule's chromophore.

- Many molecules can absorb electromagnetic radiation that is outside the visible spectrum, such as ultraviolet or infrared light, but only molecules that absorb in the visible spectrum will likely be colored.

- An auxochrome is a chemical group that, added to a chromophore, changes the wavelength where light is primarily absorbed. For example, the chemical benzene absorbs in the ultraviolet region and appears colorless. Adding a nitro group shifts the wavelength of maximum absorption to the blue region, making the compound appear yellow.

Chromophores and auxochromes result in the range of vivid colors seen in the natural and manufactured world.

SEE ALSO Colorants • Sustainable Color

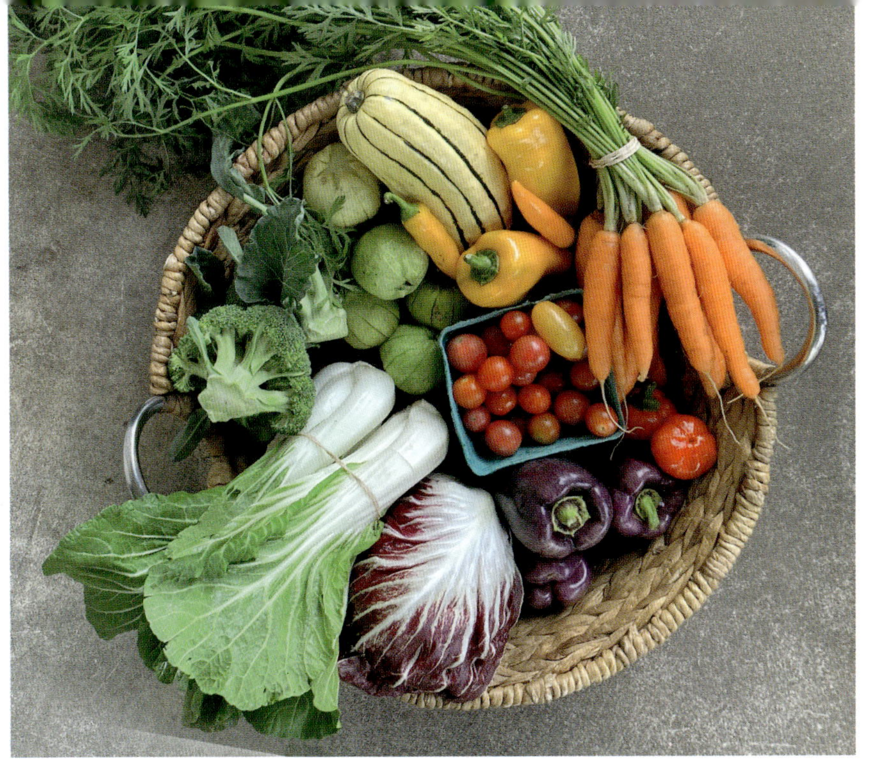

The bright colors found in many foods are caused by chromophores in natural pigments such as carotenoids (yellow, orange, and red) and anthocyanidins (red, blue, and purple).

17 CHIAROSCURO

The intentional emphasis on contrasting light and shadow

- The term *chiaroscuro* comes from the Italian: *chiaro* meaning "bright," and *scuro* meaning "dark." The technique gained prominence starting in the Renaissance, when it was widely used by Leonardo da Vinci, Rembrandt, and Caravaggio. Chiaroscuro remained popular through the Mannerist and Baroque periods.

- The Chiaroscuro movement encouraged artists to increase the contrast between light and dark in paintings, by so-called up-modeling (using mixtures with white) and down-modeling (using mixtures with black).

- Traditionally, artists preferred to use pigments in their purest form, known sometimes as a masstone. Over time, painters became more familiar with mixing either white or black with masstone pigment to create better representations of depth.

SEE ALSO Contrast • Lighting • Shadows

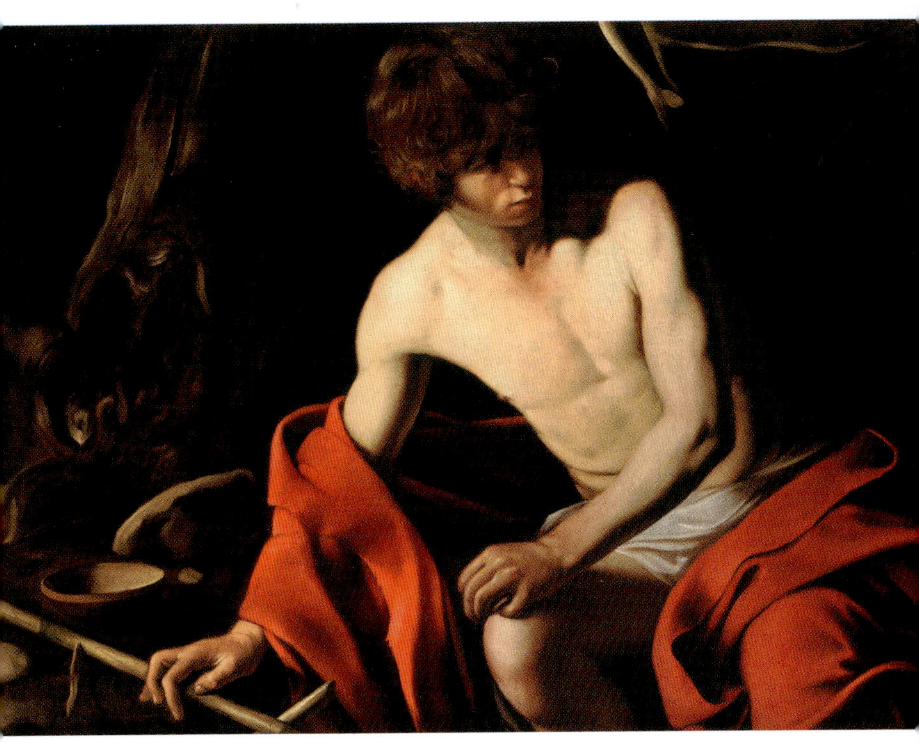

Caravaggio's *Saint John the Baptist in the Wilderness* (1605) is a prime example of the use of the chiaroscuro painting technique.

18 CHROMA

A measure of visual color strength and one of the three dimensions of color perception

- Strictly, chroma refers to a color property of objects; saturation is used to describe a related phenomenon in light sources.

- Albert Munsell's color system was based on value (also referred to as lightness), chroma, and hue. The lightness of a color at its maximum chroma varies with the hue. For example, highly chromatic yellows have high lightness, but highly chromatic blues have low lightness. The idea that perceived colors can be arranged in a sphere is a simplification of the actual shape of color perception space, which is more irregular.

Consistency in the use of the terms chroma, hue, *and* lightness *provides a systematic way to describe color in art and design.*

SEE ALSO Hue Angle • Lightness • Munsell System • Three Dimensions of Color

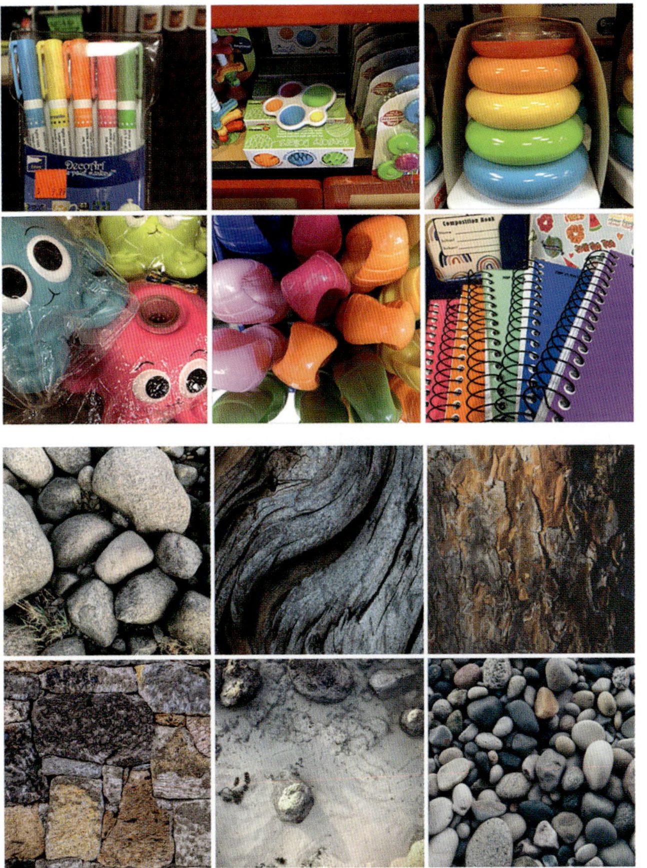

High chroma: In addition to the traditional six ROYGBV vivid hues, manufactured products in the twenty-first century now include high-chroma hues such as turquoise, lime, and magenta.

Low chroma: the natural colors of wood and stone.

19 CHROMOPHOBIA

A persistent, irrational fear of, or aversion to color

- In artist David Batchelor's book *Chromophobia*, he argues that over the centuries color has been treated as something either to fear or that is juvenile and unsophisticated.

- The misconception that classical Greek and Roman architecture and sculpture were unpainted led to a reverence for white.

- The view of color as distasteful may stem from the pre-Newtonian belief that color picks up impurities from the glass as it passes through a prism.

- Fashion designers' penchant for wearing black and persistent Hollywood images of white statues in Ancient Greece and Rome may be examples of chromophobia.

- Although a clinical phobia to color is rare, there are cases of psychological fear of, or aversion to, color. For example, a fear of red is called erythrophobia.

Chromophobia often results in an aversion to using high-chroma colors that can be seen in both designers and the public.

SEE ALSO Color Meaning • Symbolic Color

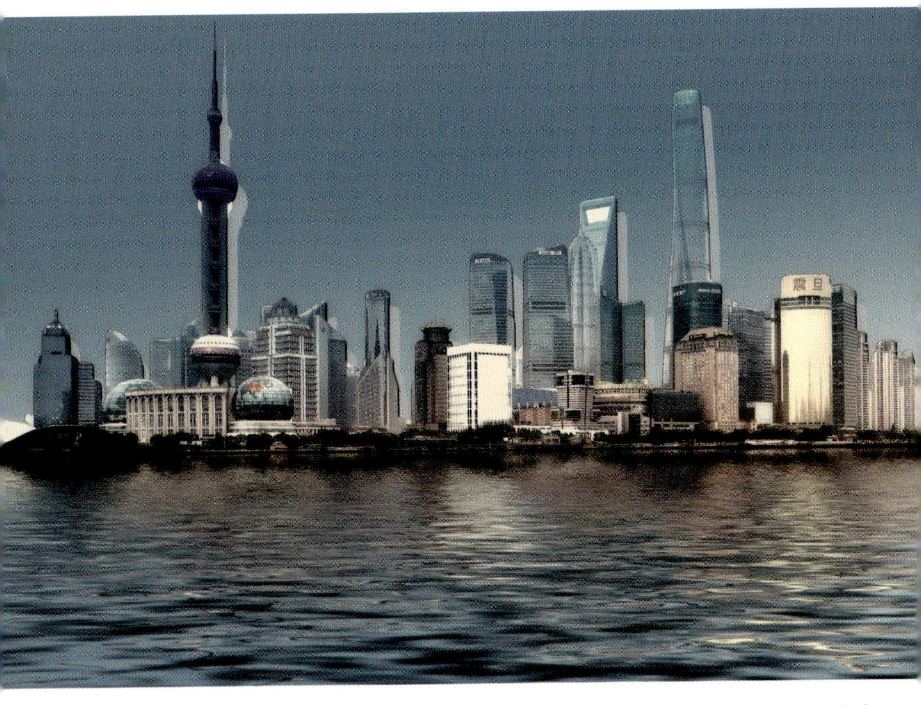

Modern cities are predominantly constructed of low-chroma building materials even though the range of colors available is greatly expanded. Why?

20 CIE SYSTEM

A system of color specification introduced by the Commission Internationale de l'Éclairage in 1931

- The CIE system was designed to determine whether two colored stimuli, such as two lights or two illuminated objects, are a visual match for an average human response.

- The main point of the system was its ability to measure the spectral reflectance or emission for a color stimulus and calculate three numbers called tristimulus values (usually referred to as XYZ values). If two stimuli have the same CIE XYZ values, they are considered a visual match for the CIE standard observer.

- In 1976, the CIE replaced the XYZ values with three new ones, referred to as L*, a*, and b*. L* represents a sample's lightness. The a* and b* values represent the redness/greenness and yellowness/blueness, respectively. CIELAB values, still widely used, are more intuitive than the XYZ versions and more useful for industrial applications.

SEE ALSO Hue Angle • Munsell System

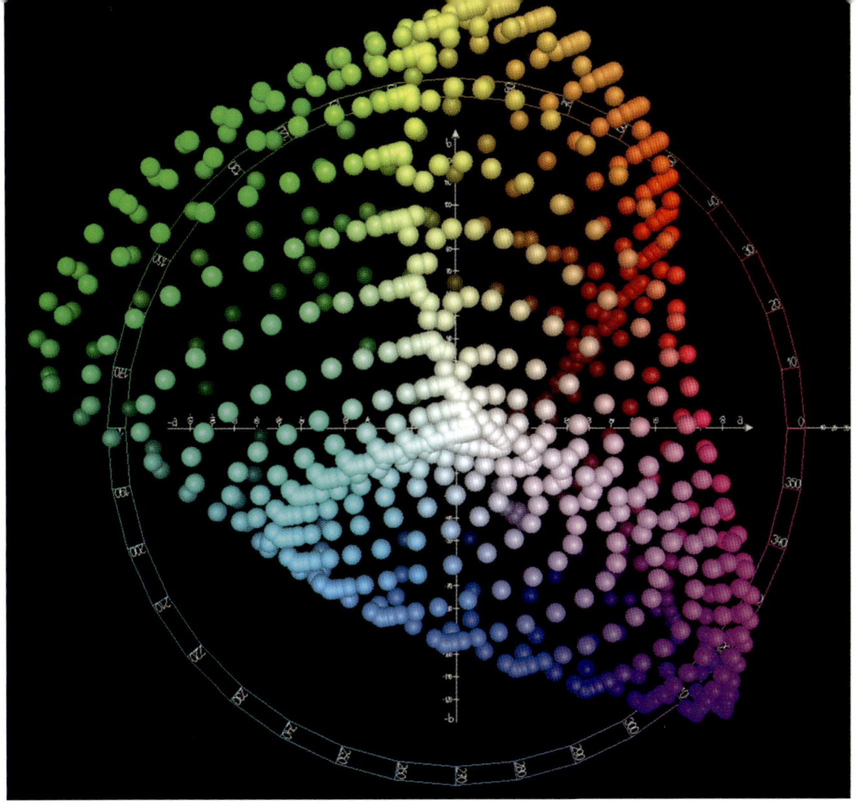

CIELAB color space from above showing a distribution of colors in the space
that can be achieved by a particular color-reproduction device.

21 CINEMATIC COLOR

Color used in cinematography to ensure that the intended atmosphere, style, or emotion is conveyed to the viewer

- A film's color script ensures that the colors of objects, clothes, and scenery convey the appropriate feel of each scene.

- Throughout the 1999 movie *The Matrix*, a dark green color wash conveys a futuristic, scientific feel. Conversely, pink provides a soft feel in the 2014 movie *The Grand Budapest Hotel*.

- Post-production color correction ensures that the colors are the ones intended by the director. Color grading is concerned primarily with the emotional feel of the movie.

Color plays a vital role in setting the atmosphere for each scene in a movie and is controlled through various processes including set composition, color correction, and color grading.

SEE ALSO Color Management • Color Meaning • Palettes

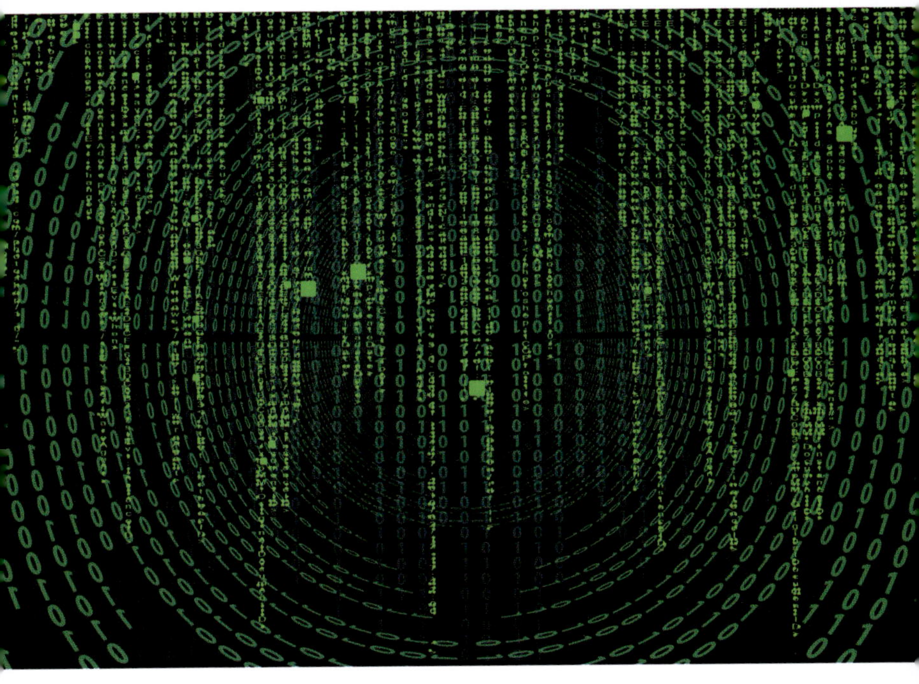

In *The Matrix* (1999) the color green was dominant throughout the movie to convey a futuristic feeling and to reinforce the idea of computer code that was traditionally written with green screens.

22 CMYK

The standard cyan, magenta, yellow, and black inks used in four-color process printing

- Printing inks are based on the optimal subtractive primaries of cyan (C), magenta (M), and yellow (Y), with black (K) added to create a four-ink system.

- Although CMYK can create a reasonable color gamut, it is nevertheless limited. High-end printing uses additional colored inks (spot colors) or multi-primary ink systems that use six or more inks.

- Because CMYK and RGB (red/green/blue) are device-dependent color spaces, there is no simple conversion formula between the two. However, color fidelity can be achieved by defining International Color Consortium (ICC) profiles. Standardization of printers and inks can allow some profiles to be predefined and used with little effort. One example is the Specifications for Web Offset Publications (SWOP) profile.

SEE ALSO Partitive Mixture • RGB • Subtractive Mixture

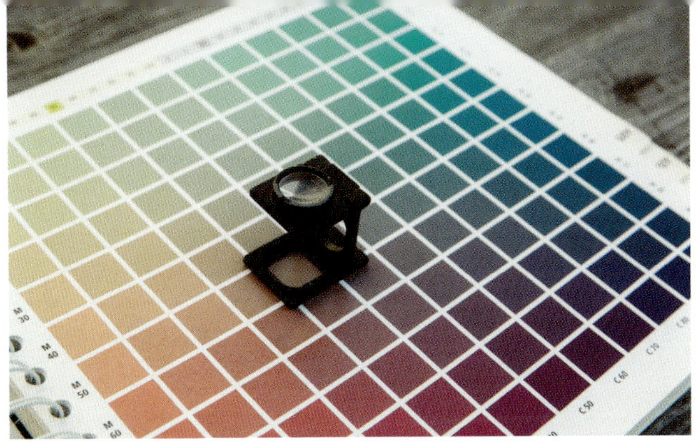

CMYK is widely used in low-cost printing systems to generate a wide range of colors.

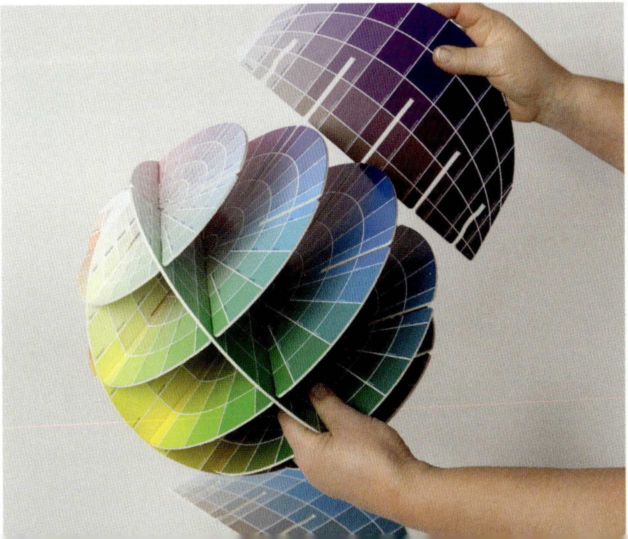

The Kolormondo model is similar to the historic Runge color sphere. It is printed using only CMY with no black.

23 COLOR CONSTANCY

The tendency to perceive a familiar object as having the same color when viewed under different conditions of illumination

- We see an object's color as a result of visual processes in response to light that is reflected from or emitted by it. An object viewed under a bluish light source reflects more blue light to the eye than the same object viewed under a reddish light source of the same intensity.

- The color of most objects changes in appearance as the light source is changed. For example, sand on the beach may look a little redder at sunset than at noon. However, the change is much smaller than we might expect, due to a visual process called color constancy by which objects tend to retain their approximate daylight appearance when viewed under a wide range of light sources.

- Our perception of the color of unfamiliar objects is influenced by assumptions of illumination based on experience.

The visual system has evolved so that we can easily and quickly recognize objects by their color appearance regardless of the lighting in which they are viewed.

SEE ALSO #TheDress • Context

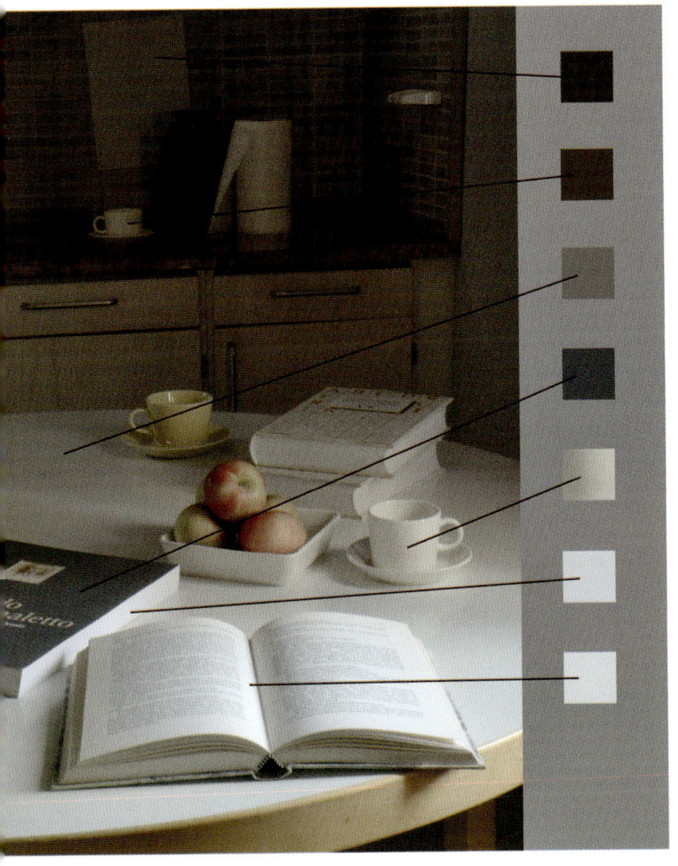

Many variations of white and one of gray. Note the difference in the appearance of the two coffee cups. How do you know they are the same color?

24 COLOR FIELD PAINTING

A style of abstract painting that emerged in New York City in the 1950s, characterized by large areas of color

- The term *color field painter* was coined by art critic Clement Greenberg and originally applied to three prominent artists: Mark Rothko, Barnett Newman, and Clyfford Still. The style was a type of abstract expressionism that aimed to strip away suggestions of recognizable forms and express raw emotion through color.

- In many of these paintings, foreground and background are one and consist mainly of a single uniform hue, typically applied to a huge canvas. Still was arguably the first to arrive at this new style, applying rich earthy hues in thick layers to the canvas using a palette knife.

- In the 1960s, other artists including Helen Frankenthaler, Sam Gilliam, and John Hoyland adopted the style in an even more abstract way.

SEE ALSO Albers's *Interaction of Color* • International Klein Blue • Op Art

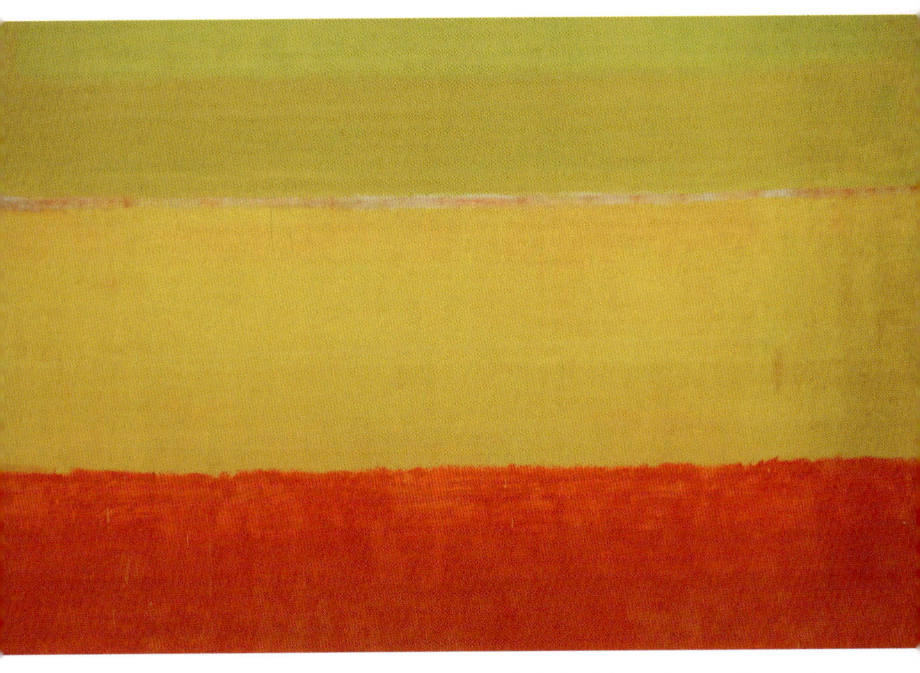

Untitled (1952-53), a painting by Mark Rothko juxtaposing large areas of color. Another painting, *White Center* (1950), was sold at auction by Sotheby's for $73 million in 2007.

25 COLOR FORECASTING

The marketing process of selecting colors that are likely to sell well in upcoming seasons

- Forecasts are made by groups of color consultants from specific industries who work together to collect data, anticipate cultural trends, and predict product colors that will be popular with consumers in the future. They work from one to two years in advance for fashion and up to five years for the automotive industry.

- Color forecasting for product categories expanded in the 1960s. The focus on a single new color dates to 2000, when Pantone announced its first Color of the Year.

- There is growing concern about the accuracy of the forecasting process and that products that cannot be sold contribute to overconsumption and waste.

SEE ALSO Brand Colors • Color Meaning • Colorways • Pantone

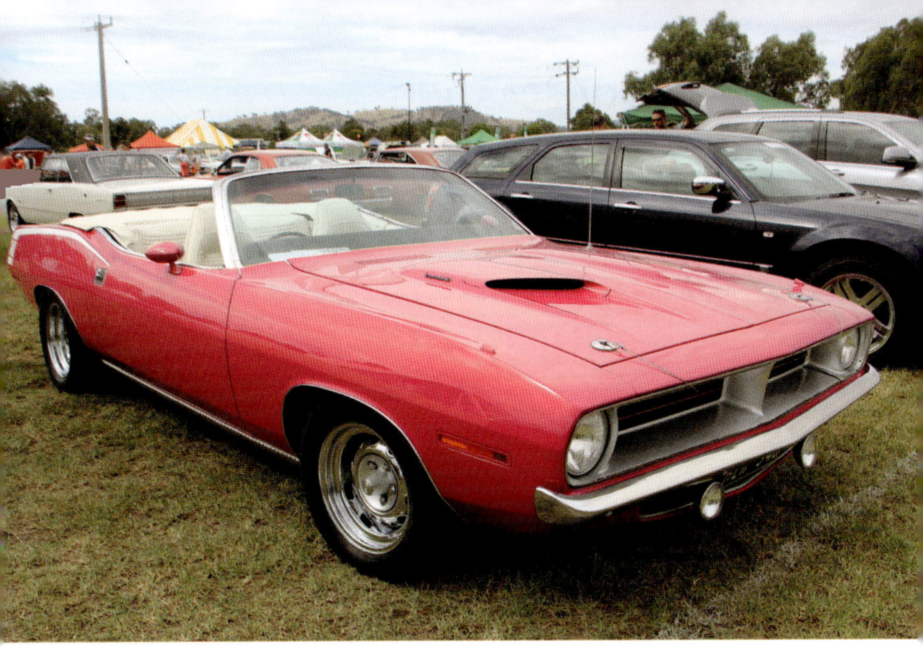

Advances in color chemistry are partly driven by the auto industry. Panther Pink and Moulin Rouge were the "hot" colors in 1970 for American muscle cars.

26 COLOR LITERACY

The ability to use color effectively through knowledge, competence, and practical application

- Color literacy closes the gap between the scientific understanding of color and the traditional approach to color practiced in art education.

- Color literacy includes a growing awareness that color's impact is cultural and environmental as well as aesthetic.

- There is growing interest in STEAM education, which adds the arts to the STEM disciplines of science, technology, engineering, and mathematics. Color is an ideal STEAM subject that can introduce children to exploration, observation, and critical thinking.

- The Colour Literacy Project is exploring ways to improve the quality of color education through a curriculum that combines science literacy and visual literacy.

SEE ALSO Human Visual System • Perception Triangle

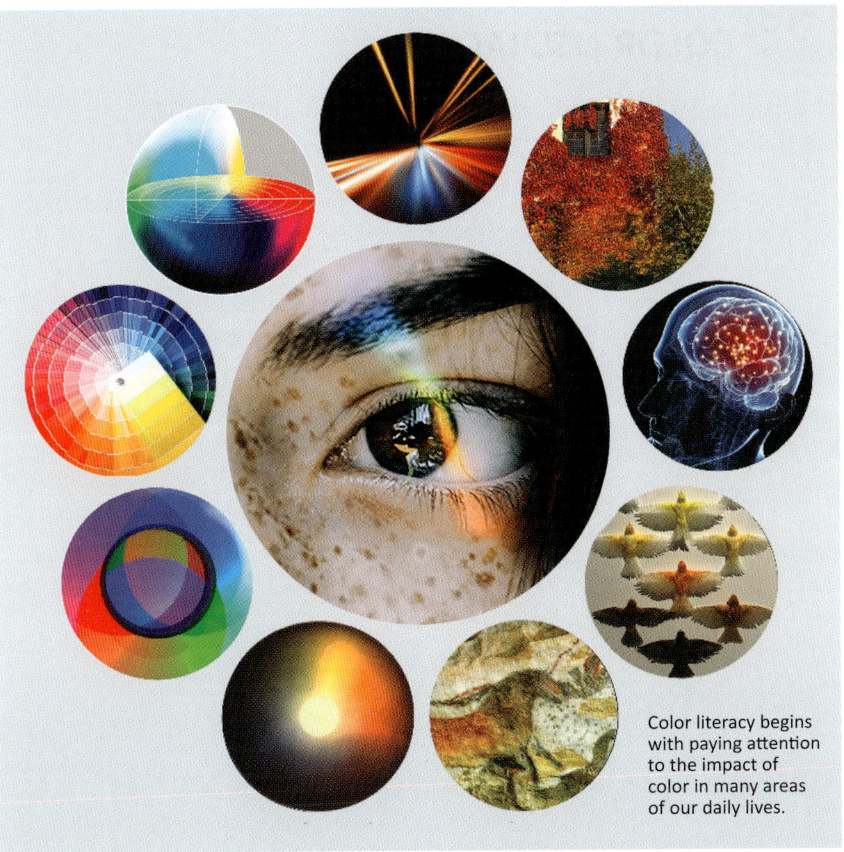

Color literacy begins with paying attention to the impact of color in many areas of our daily lives.

27 COLOR MANAGEMENT

The process of aligning color specifications across devices to ensure color fidelity

- Emissive displays generate colors by combining light from three primary sources, usually red, green, and blue. Digital color is represented by three numbers (RGB) at each pixel position in the image. The RGB values for any particular device must be adjusted to ensure consistent color generation.

- Color printers use colorants that absorb light. The optimal process primaries are cyan (red-absorbing), magenta (green-absorbing), and yellow (blue-absorbing). Most printers also use black (CMYK).

- Operating systems and applications enable color fidelity through profiles created by the International Color Consortium (ICC), but perfect fidelity is hard to achieve because each imaging device has a limited color gamut.

Color management is an imperfect but vital process that helps ensure color fidelity in reproduction.

SEE ALSO CMYK • Color Measurement • Gamuts • RGB

Standardized calibration charts, such as the classic Macbeth ColorChecker, can be used to build an International Color Consortium (ICC) profile for a device.

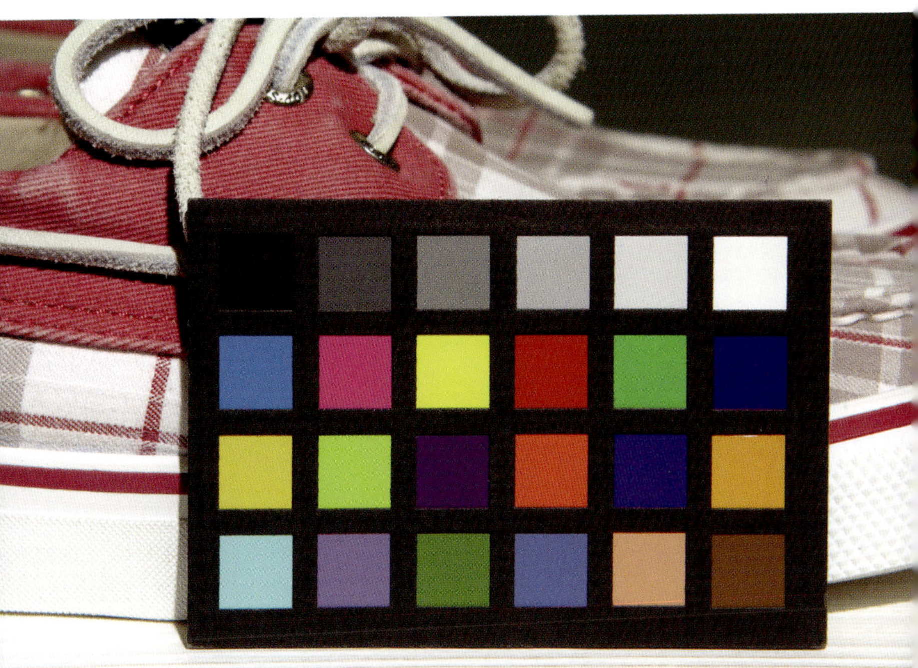

28 COLOR MEANING

Color is used to communicate ideas and concepts through cultural associations and psychological effects

- Response to color involves many aspects of experience, including cognitive, emotional, behavioral, physiological, spiritual, and linguistic. Response to the same color can vary with the context; for example, we may like to wear a particular color but would not use it on a wall in our homes.

- We often associate specific colors with specific objects, as in blue with sky. Categories also convey meaning. For example, dark colors are typically considered strong, pale colors delicate, and vivid colors intense.

Color meanings are arguably as important as color aesthetics for the successful use of color in art, design, and packaging. Effective color design is often achieved when the meanings communicated by the colors are consistent with the meanings expressed by the typography, imagery, and content.

SEE ALSO Symbolic Color • Three Dimensions of Color • Warm and Cool

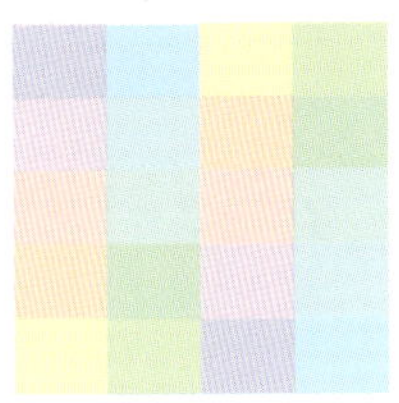

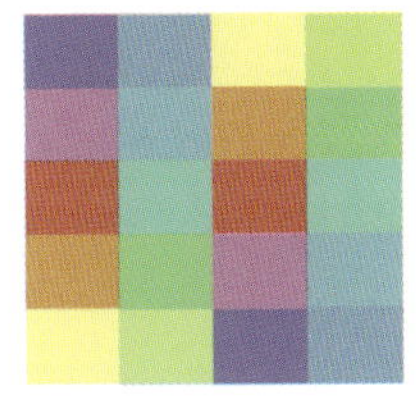

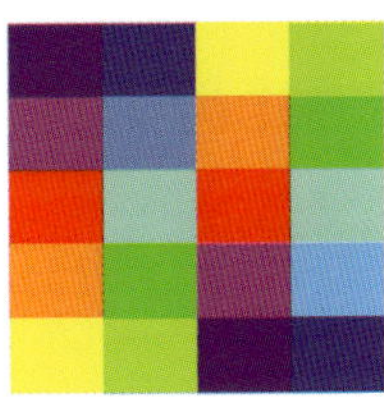

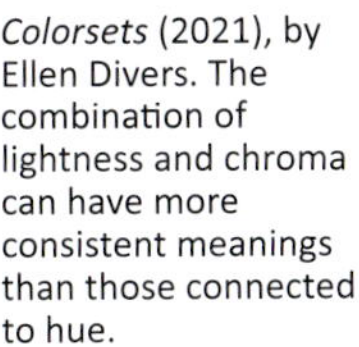

Colorsets (2021), by Ellen Divers. The combination of lightness and chroma can have more consistent meanings than those connected to hue.

LIGHT CHROMA
Light
Soft
Delicate
Relaxed
Young
Friendly

MEDIUM CHROMA
Cheerful
Friendly
Energetic
Young
Light

HIGH CHROMA
Energetic
Strong
Cheerful
Friendly
Intense
Hard

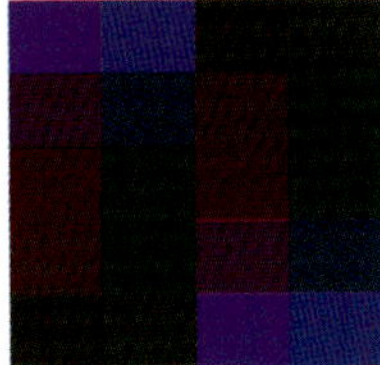

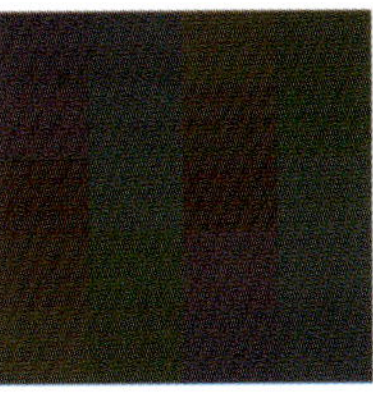

MEDIUM NEUTRAL
Light
Soft
Calm
Delicate
Relaxed

DARK CHROMA
Heavy
Strong
Hard
Mature
Serious

DARK NEUTRAL
Serious
Mature
Heavy
Strong
Aloof
Hard
Intense
Calm

29 COLOR MEASUREMENT

The practice of instrumental measurement and specification of color

- The science of colorimetry, which uses three numbers to specify a color, dates from the early twentieth century. In the CIE system of colorimetry, adopted in 1931, three numbers, called tristimulus values, specify color. They can be calculated by measuring reflected, emitted, or transmitted light and are represented by the letters XYZ.

- If two color stimuli have the same XYZ values, they will be a color match when viewed by an average observer. In manufacturing, this provides an objective way to determine whether a production sample matches the color standard provided by a client.

Affordable instruments are available and being used for color communication by designers in interior and architectural applications.

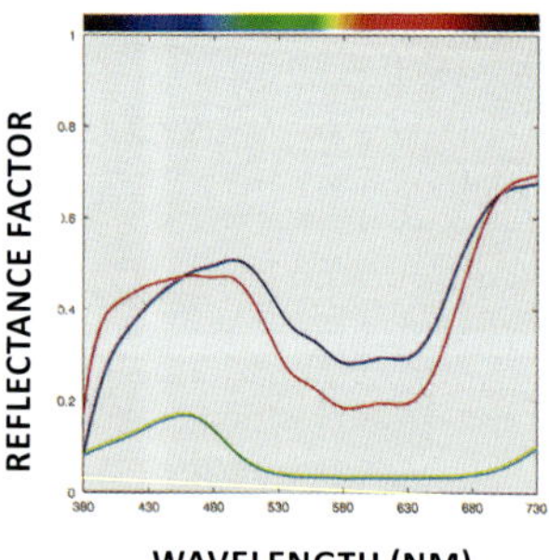

The three spectral curves above show measurements taken of the left side door for three different bedroom paintings by Van Gogh. The data collected provided information about the pigments used for each painting.

SEE ALSO CIE System • Color Management • Electromagnetic Spectrum

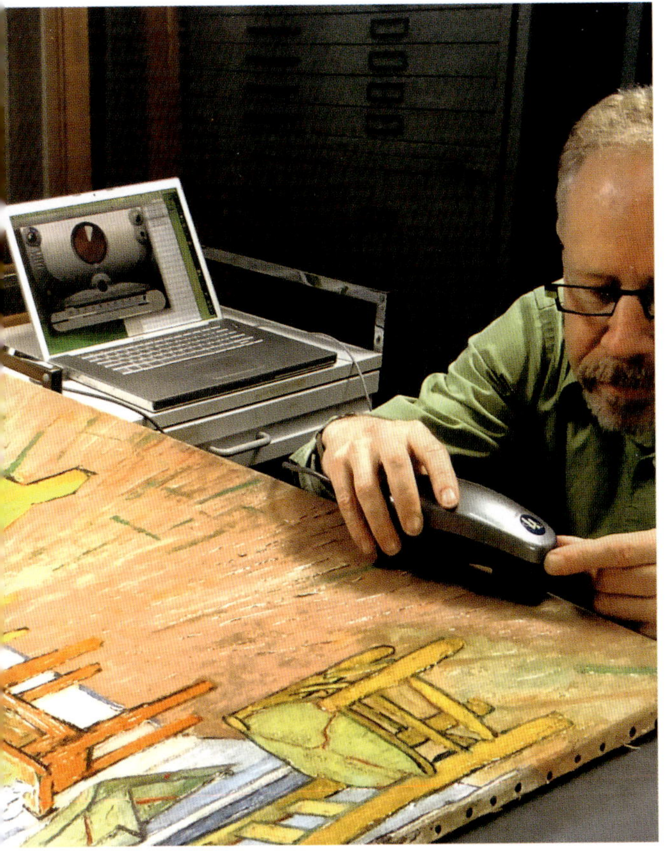

Color scientist Roy Berns measured three of the bedroom paintings by Van Gogh as part of a conservation program.

30 COLOR ORDER SYSTEMS

Systematic methods of arranging colors for specification

- Hues were first arranged in a circle by Isaac Newton. Many 3D arrangements followed, beginning with a spherical version published by Philip Otto Runge in 1810.

- Today we distinguish between conceptual color order systems and those that can also be physically realized. Munsell is perhaps the best-known physical system. By contrast, CIELAB is a mathematical construct. Both systems are helpful because they allow colors to be referred to by the position they occupy in the space.

- The German RAL design system and the Swedish Natural Color System (NCS) system are two modern examples of successful commercial color order systems.

Color order systems are widely used as color communication tools in fashion, interior design, and graphic design.

SEE ALSO Munsell System • Natural Color System

THREE PROPRIETARY SYSTEMS

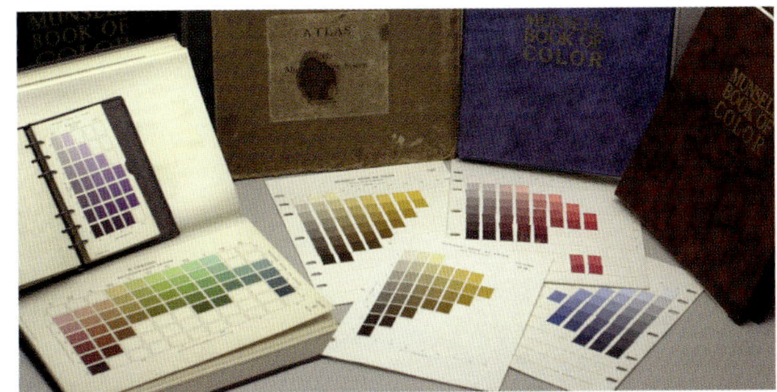

The Munsell system, a 3D system devised by Albert H. Munsell, was designed to have samples that were arranged so that the steps between the samples were perceptually equal. Notation: Hue, Value, Chroma (Vivid Yellow = 5Y 8.5/14).

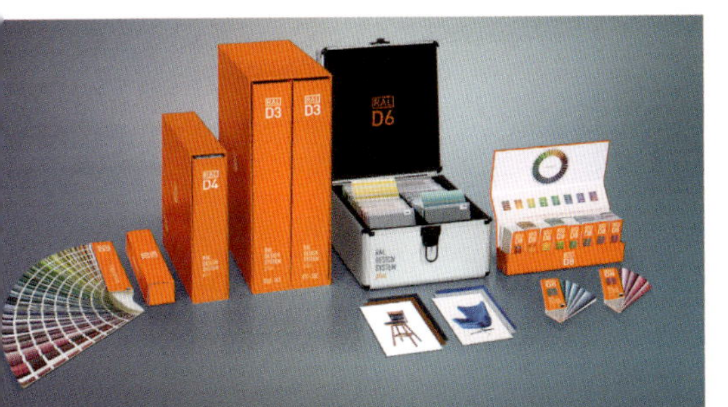

The German RAL system, based on CIELAB, defines colors for paints, coatings, and plastics. Notation: Lightness, Chroma, Hue Angle (Vivid Yellow = 085 80 85).

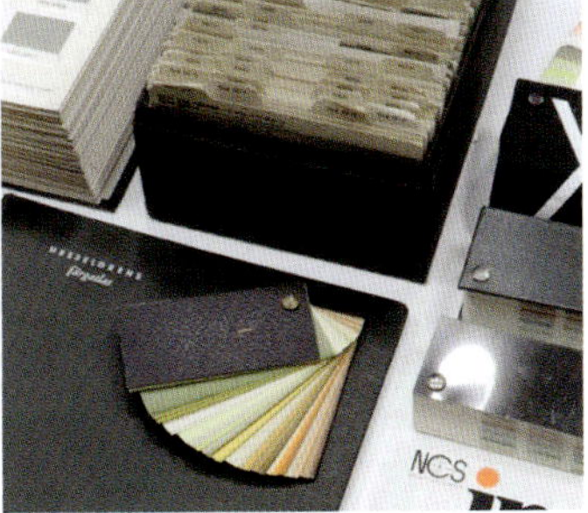

The Swedish Natural Color System is based on the color opponency hypothesis of color vision first proposed by Ewald Hering. Notation: Blackness, Chromaticness, Hue (Vivid Yellow = S 0080-Y).

31 COLOR SCALES

A sequence of colors illustrating the steps between two colors

- Color scales can be made in any media to illustrate the range of colors possible between two specific colors. Both physical and digital media offer strategies to add graduations between the steps.

- Types of color scales include:

  - Gray, or achromatic, scales show steps (usually eight to 10) between black and white.

  - Hue, or chromatic, scales, show steps between two colors of different hues.

  - Lightness, or value, scales show steps between any color and black and/or white, or how a specific hue steps to both black and to white.

  - Chroma scales show steps between any color and gray. Usually it is between a color and gray of the same value, or lightness level, but a scale can also show the colors between a specific color and a middle gray.

SEE ALSO Gradients • Tint, Shade, and Tone

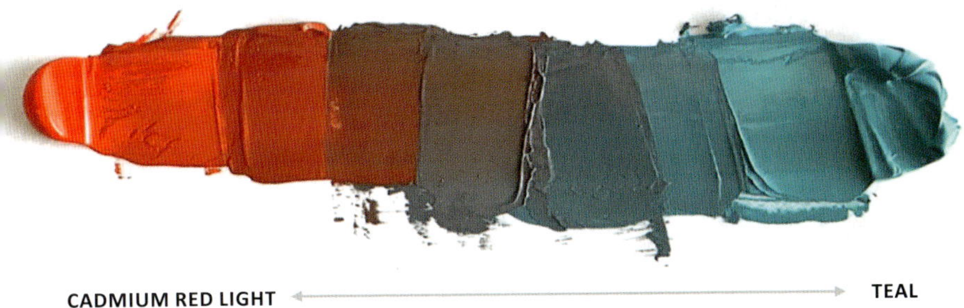

Chromatic acrylic paint scale from red to teal
(Golden paint company).

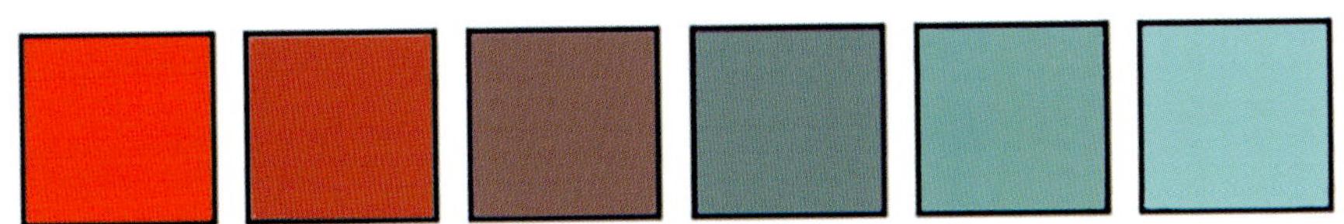

Digital scale from red to teal.

32 COLOR SCHEMES

A limited selection of colors chosen intentionally to create a work of art or design

- A color scheme can be created using formulaic types of harmony, such as monochromatic (all the colors have the same hue), complementary (the colors have opposite hues), and split-complementary (one color plus a complementary color on either side). Many other factors contribute to a successful color scheme including the lightness key, chroma levels, placement, and proportion.

- A color scheme can be chosen from a painting such as Sonia Delaunay's *Prismes Électriques*, which includes many low-chroma colors to balance the vivid hues.

- Sometimes the terms *color palette* and *color scheme* are used interchangeably, but a palette is a larger set from which to pick colors to create color schemes.

The combination of lightness and chroma are as important as hue selection in setting the tone of a color scheme.

SEE ALSO Color Meaning • Gamuts • Palettes

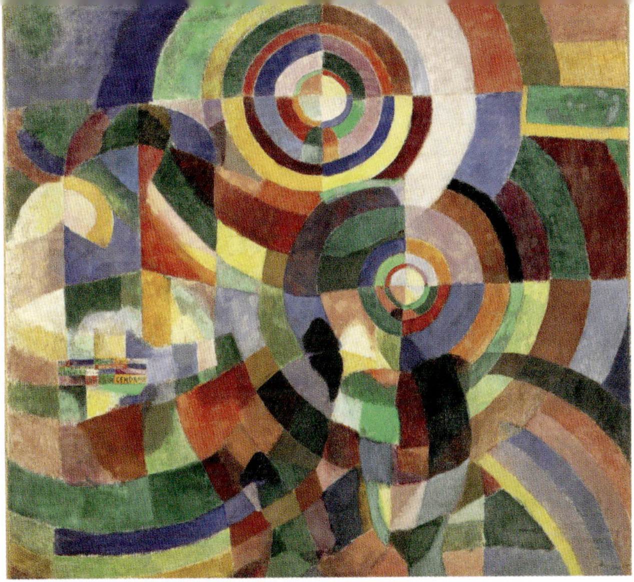

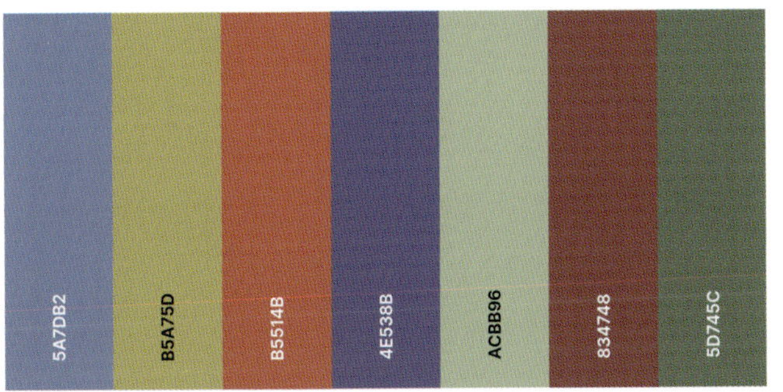

Prismes Électriques (1914), oil painting by Sonia Delaunay.

How would you define this digitally extracted color scheme of Sonia Delaunay's painting?

33 COLOR TEMPERATURE

A measurement used to describe the color appearance of a light source

- Color temperature measurement is based on a theoretical construct developed by physicist Max Planck in the early 1900s in which an object called a black body emits radiation as it is heated. As the temperature increases, the spectral distribution of the emitted radiation changes. At low temperatures it contains more long wavelengths and looks warm; at high temperatures it contains more short wavelengths and looks cool.

- Correlated color temperature (CCT), designated by the Kelvin temperature scale (K), is used to characterize a light source. Candlelight has a CCT of about 2,000K, incandescent light about 3,000K, and daylight about 6,500K.

The ability to adjust color temperature is an ongoing area of research in the lighting industry as well as a critical consideration in designing interior spaces at home and in the workplace.

SEE ALSO LED Color • Lighting

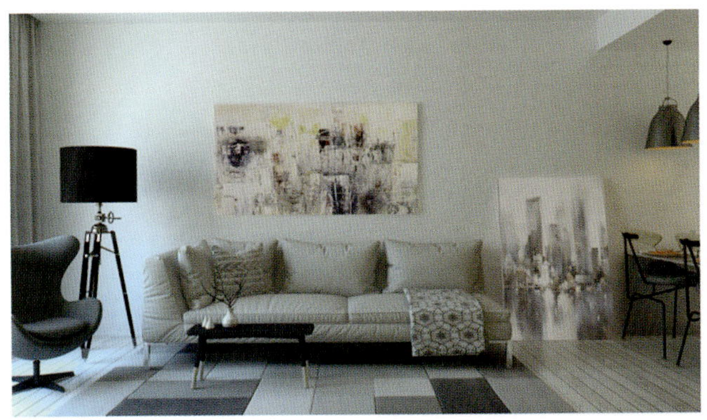

The same scene illuminated by lights of high CCT (upper) and low CCT (lower). Notice the very different feel of the room in each case.

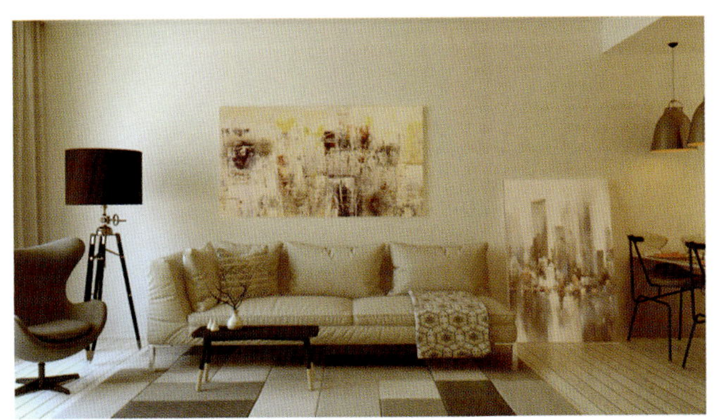

34 COLORANTS

A material that can impart color, such as dyes and pigments

- Organic colorants are based on molecules that contain the element carbon. Inorganic colorants are generally based on minerals and usually have better light fastness.

- A dye is applied in a solution. A material is dipped into it, and the dye typically binds to the fiber, imparting a stable color. A pigment is an insoluble compound, often applied as a suspension in a medium such as a polymer that hardens as it dries, forming a durable layer.

- Dyes are typically used on textiles, and pigments to color paints and plastics. Printing inks sometimes use pigments, but more often dyes.

- Both dyes and pigments impart color primarily by selectively absorbing some wavelengths of light more than others. For example, a yellow dye absorbs shorter wavelengths more than the longer ones, which are reflected to the eye and perceived as color.

SEE ALSO Black and White • Chemistry of Chromophores • International Klein Blue

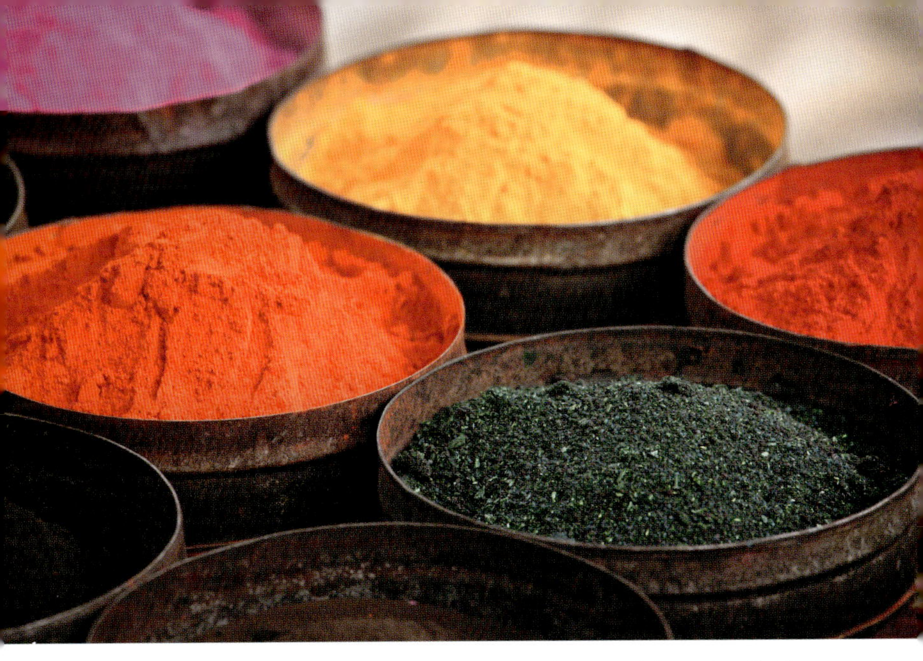

Whereas dyes are soluble and applied from a solution, pigments are typically suspended in a medium when they are applied (e.g., in a paint). Pigments are identified by numbers. See the online Color of Art Pigment Database.

35 COLORWAYS

Different combinations of colors in which a design can be produced

- The use of different colorways enables the same pattern or design to be reproduced in many ways. The choice of colorway can dramatically change the feel of a design. Research has shown that different colorways can change how people perceive the forms or shapes within a design.

- Typically, a designer produces a printed design on paper or textile in three or four different colorways. These can be implemented in digital printing processes or produced in woven fabric.

- Digital computer-aided design (CAD) software has become ubiquitous in design education and commercial design operations because it allows designers to explore different colorways quickly and effortlessly.

SEE ALSO Bezold Effect • Color Schemes • Palettes

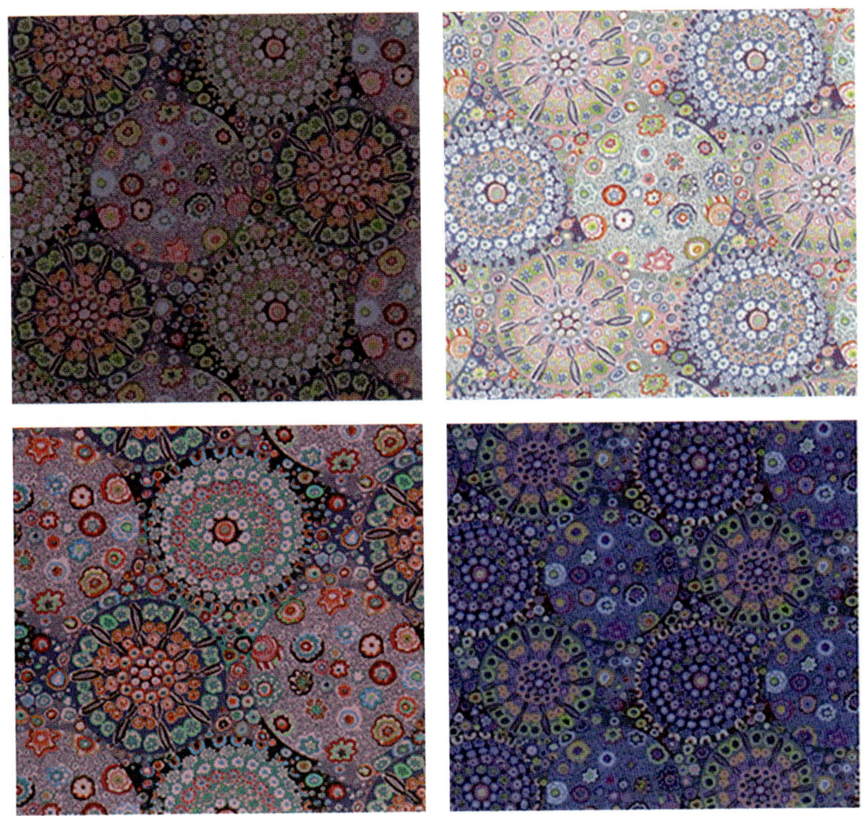

Millefiore fabric by Kaffe Fassett. The same design is illustrated using four different colorways.

36 COMPLEMENTARY COLORS

Hues that are opposite to each other in some sense

- Sometimes complementary colors (hues) are said to be those that are opposite each other on the color wheel, but not all wheels show the same hues as complementary.

- Afterimage colors are sometimes called optical complements. If we stare at a vivid swatch for a time, then stare at a neutral color, we will often perceive a color that is the visual opposite of the original color. The Impressionists placed colors with maximum contrast side by side to create the most vivid visual color sensations.

- In mixing terminology, complementary colors are ones that neutralize each other, but whether two colorants can be mixed to create an approximate neutral depends on their spectral properties, not just on their appearance.

Which hue opposes which other hue is more complicated than is often presented in traditional color theory.

SEE ALSO Subtractive Mixture • Successive Contrast

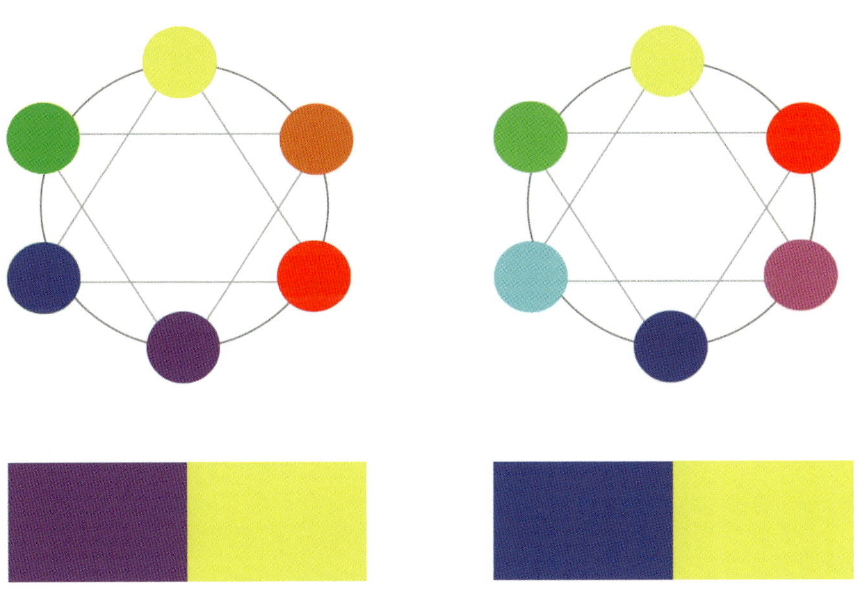

Six-hue color wheels based on a subtractive RYB system (left) and an additive RGB system (right). Notice blue is opposite to orange in one system and opposite to yellow in the other system. Do we get maximum contrast when blue is placed next to orange or next to yellow?

37 CONTEXT

Colors are almost always seen in context, surrounded by colors that affect their appearance

- Color perception is relative. The color that we see when we look at an object, or part of it, depends on the context—that is, the effects of the surrounding colors. These effects are described by terms such as *simultaneous contrast* and *assimilation*.

- Even the spectral colors we see when we look at individual wavelengths of light depend on the colors against which they are viewed. Other phenomena such as memory color can also affect color perception.

SEE ALSO Atmospheric Perspective • Bezold Effect • Simultaneous Contrast • Successive Contrast

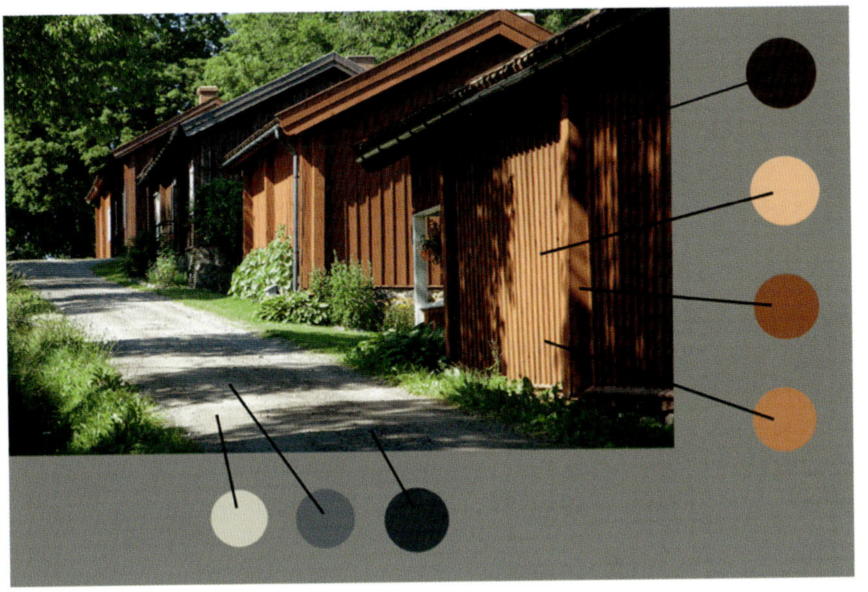

Unrelated colors seen through a tube are like a palette for re-creating the image. We perceive and experience many levels of color simultaneously: We apprehend the uniform red-earth coloring of the houses and the grayness of the gravel road. At the same time, we perceive the colors' modulation in light, shadow, and space.

38 CONTRAST

The amount of difference in the color appearance of colored lights and surfaces compared with adjacent colors.

- One of the earliest references to contrast was by the physicist Ibn al-Haytham (965–1040), who noticed that spots of paint on a white background looked blacker than their "true" color.

- Mechanisms in the eye and cognitive processes in the brain both contribute toward contrast.

- Temporal, or successive, contrast can occur when color appearance contrasts with what has previously been seen, causing the phenomenon of afterimages.

Consideration of contrast enables artists and designers to enhance the effect of color combinations. Lightness contrast is the most important consideration for legibility, while hue and chroma contrasts provide additional opportunities for visual emphasis.

SEE ALSO Complementary Colors • Simultaneous Contrast • Successive Contrast

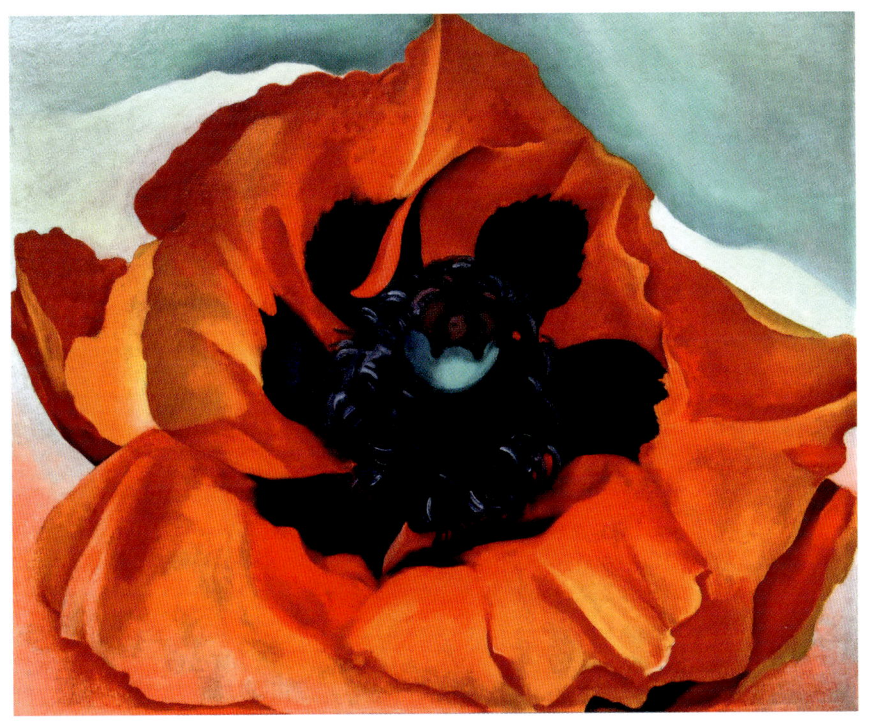

Poppy (1927), high-contrast oil painting by Georgia O'Keeffe.

39 ELECTROMAGNETIC SPECTRUM

The range of wavelengths or frequencies over which electromagnetic radiation extends

- Electromagnetic radiation is characterized by wavelengths, which vary enormously. An FM radio station broadcasting at 90 MHz has a wavelength of 3.3 meters, while that of gamma rays is about 100 picometres (a picometre is one-trillionth of a meter).

- Our visual systems are sensitive to electromagnetic radiation in the range of roughly 360 to 780 nanometers (nm). One nm is one-billionth of a meter. In certain conditions some humans are sensitive to wavelengths as short as 300 nm and as long as 1,000 nm.

- Some insects such as bees are sensitive to ultraviolet (UV) light and can see patterns on flowers that are invisible to humans. Bats and mosquitoes have visual sensitivity extending into the infrared (IR) range.

- All electromagnetic radiation, including light, has aspects of both a wave and a particle, called a photon. As the photon size increases, the radiation becomes more hazardous. Radiation with wavelengths less than about 400 nm is dangerous, and gamma rays are life-threatening.

- Wave-particle duality is an essential component of quantum mechanics.

SEE ALSO CIE System • Color Measurement • Spectral Hues

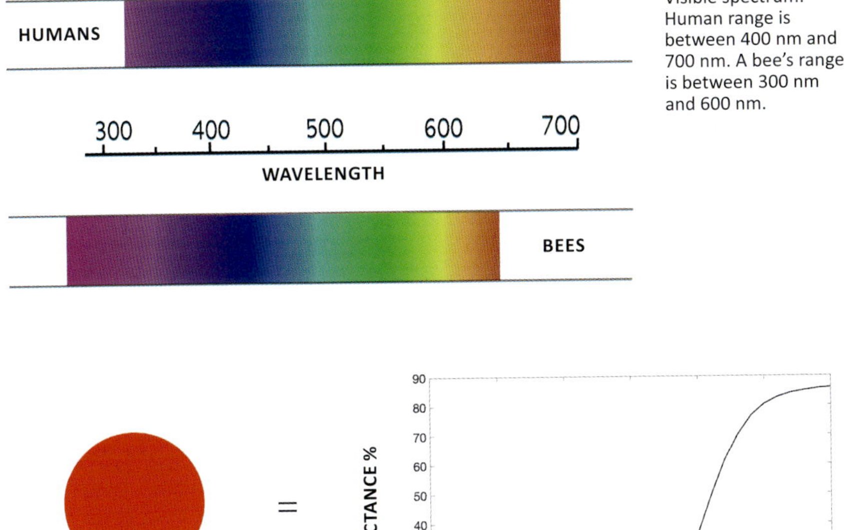

Spectral reflectance curve: a graphical representation of the amount of light that an object reflects at each wavelength in the visible spectrum.

40 EMOTION AND COLOR

Color is historically thought to have an affective response that is linked to human emotion

- In the past century popular psychology reinforced the notion of a direct correspondence between vivid hues and people's emotions, based on the theory that each basic emotion, such as joy, anger, and fear, had its own neural pathway in the brain. This paradigm failed to address less intense responses that people have to everyday events, places, people, and objects.

- Research on color and emotion has ranged from measuring physiological responses, such as heart rate and blood pressure, to observing behavior, to recording subjects' verbal or written responses. However, methodological concerns have made it difficult to arrive at solid conclusions.

- Studies have typically focused on chromatic hues and neglected the many variations in lightness and chroma that exist within a hue. Also, colors are typically studied one at a time, which does not explain their effect when experienced in combination with other colors.

- Researchers are beginning to address these issues, so clearer answers about color and emotion may be forthcoming.

SEE ALSO Character Zones • Color Meaning • Symbolism

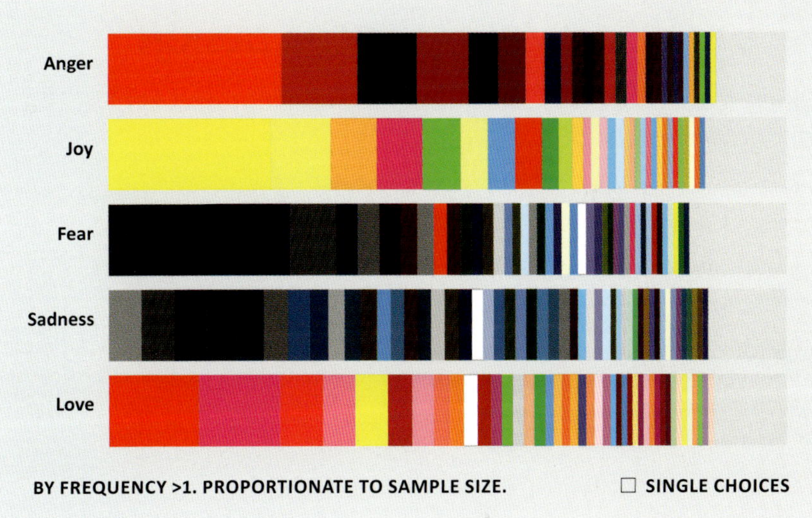

Color associations of 250 participants, part of Emotionally}Vague, a visual research project by Orlagh O'Brien conducted worldwide between 2006 and 2012.

41 ENVIRONMENTAL COLOR DESIGN

Design focused on the intentional use of color and light in the built environment

- Environmental design includes architecture, landscape design, urban planning, interior design, industrial design, graphic design, textile design, and fashion design.

- Environmental color design involves the intentional use of color to support and enhance the design objectives.

- Colored environments and lighting can influence physical responses in both positive and negative ways. Research on the range and degree of environmental effects of color and light on human emotions, cognition, and behavior is ongoing.

SEE ALSO Geography of Color • Sustainable Color

CMF DESIGN

Color, Materials, and Finish (CMF) design is an area of industrial design that focuses on the chromatic, tactile, and surface appearance of products and environments.

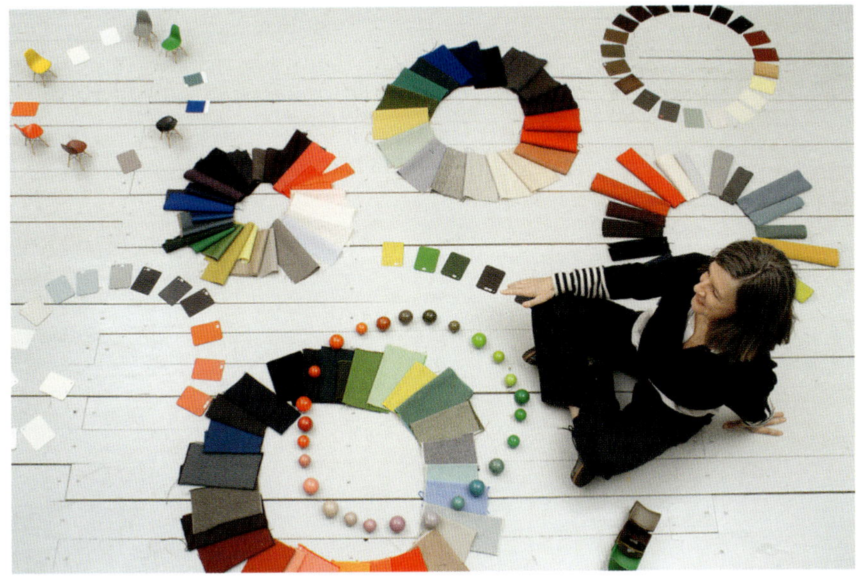

Industrial designer Hella Jongerius working on the color design for Vitra Colour.

42 FLAT COLOR

Color that is solid and completely uniform with no gradations or shading

- Examples of flat color can be found throughout history in the decorative arts, illustration and graphic arts, animation and digital arts, as well as fine arts. The hallmark of mid-century graphic design, solid color, is the main feature of the flat design trend.

- Flat color was used to produce posters, cartoons, and comic strips as early as the mid-1800s. The style was firmly established by the late 1920s with the release of animated films that used flat art for the painted cells.

- The earliest color comics were printed using screens cut for each color. The expense of manually cutting the screens resulted in a limited palette. Today, "flatting"—filling in areas of line art with flat color—is done digitally by a professional "flatter," and the color choices are infinite. Depending on the style of the creator, comics and graphic novels can be published as flat color or highly rendered by a colorist.

The use of flat color is a stylistic choice for artists and graphic designers.

SEE ALSO Gradients

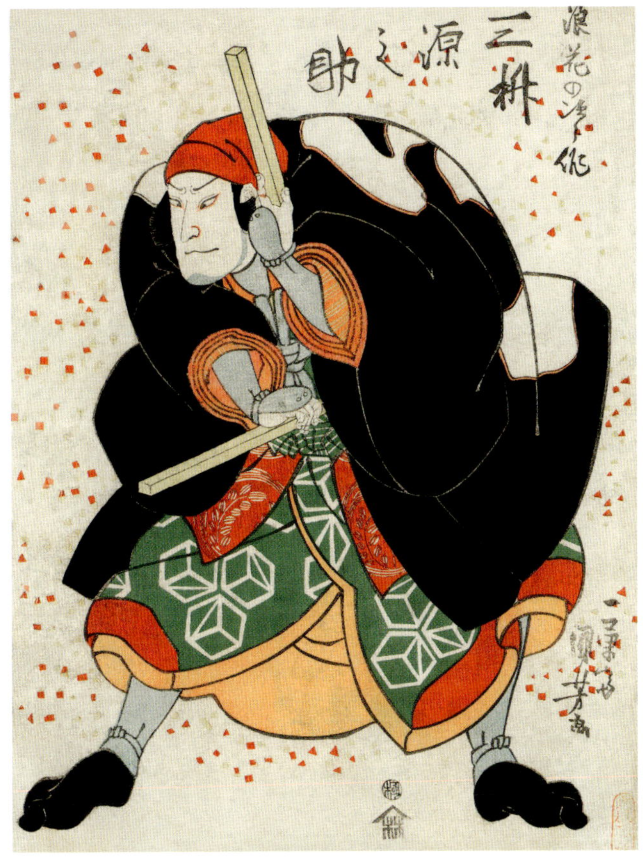

Woodblock print (c. 1830), by Utagawa Kuniyoshi. When Japan reopened trade with the West in 1854, the flat color of Japanese woodblock prints became a source of inspiration for artists of the late 1800s.

43 FLUORESCENCE

The property of absorbing light at one wavelength and emitting it at a longer wavelength

- Fluorescence is an important aspect of many lighting systems. While fluorescent tubes are increasingly being replaced by LED lighting systems, even some of these use fluorescence as a way to achieve a light source with better color-rendering properties.

- Consumers are familiar with fluorescence through its use in clothing and plastic materials to create safety clothing and signs. Frequently, fluorescent materials absorb in the nonvisible region of the spectrum and emit light in the visible region. This can create colors that are very vivid and highly chromatic.

- Although fluorescence is often considered to be an artificial phenomenon, some materials (even human teeth!) exhibit fluorescence naturally.

- A related phenomenon was used to create the neon lights used to illuminate cities beginning in the 1930s. With neon lighting there is no actual fluorescence. Rather, the neon gas emits light when electricity is passed through the electrodes in the neon-filled glass tube.

SEE ALSO Human Visual System • Safety Colors

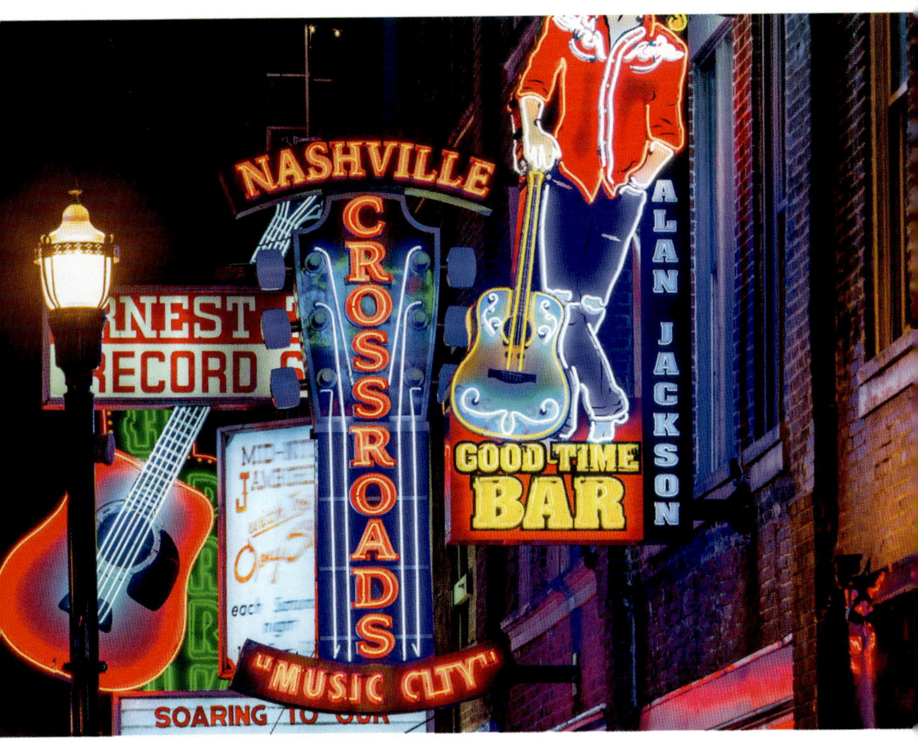

In a related phenomenon, neon lighting shines on lower Broadway in Nashville.

44 GAMUTS

The range of colors that can be created by a colorant or a color-forming system

- While it is not possible to generate all possible colors from three primaries, it is possible to create all hues—though not all at high chroma.

- The gamut of a typical RGB (red/green/blue) display is defined by a triangle in chromaticity space. It is impossible to generate colors outside of the RGB system's triangular gamut.

- The gamut of a typical CMYK (cyan/magenta/yellow/black) process printer is smaller than the gamut of a digital display.

- The gamut of colors possible in a painting is dependent on the specific pigments selected for the primary colors.

In any color mixing system, if a small set of colors is carefully selected, it is possible to generate a wide range of colors, but not all high-chroma colors.

SEE ALSO CMYK • Palettes • RGB

GAMUT MAPPING

This gamut map by James Gurney shows the area of the color wheel that is defined by boundary lines between the three paint primaries of yellow ochre, Venetian red, and ultramarine blue used in his painting.

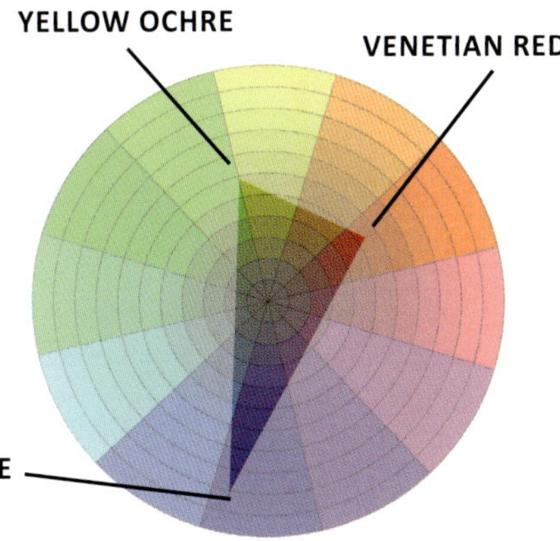

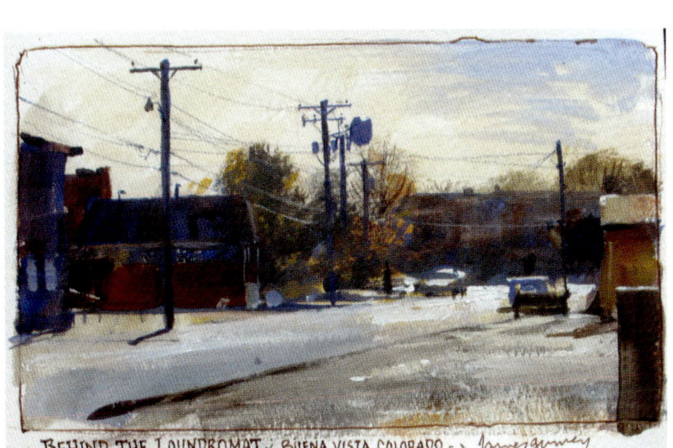

Behind the Laundromat, a painting by James Gurney illustrating the narrow gamut produced by using yellow ochre, Venetian Red, and ultramarine blue.

45 GEOGRAPHY OF COLOR

The influence of local materials, climate, and traditional construction techniques on the chromatic character of vernacular architecture around the world

- Based on the color analysis method developed by Jean-Philippe and Dominique Lenclos, the geography of color refers to the variations found in specific parts of the world where the use of color in the built environment depends on the local climate and availability of building materials, as well as the cultural traditions and belief systems of the area.

- People develop deep connections to places based on the characteristics of the natural and built environments, how they interact with them, and how their surroundings make them feel. In areas with a strong chromatic sense of place, the use of color can either enhance or diminish it.

Awareness of the site-specific geography of color can both inspire and inform design decisions.

SEE ALSO Environmental Color Design • Sustainable Color

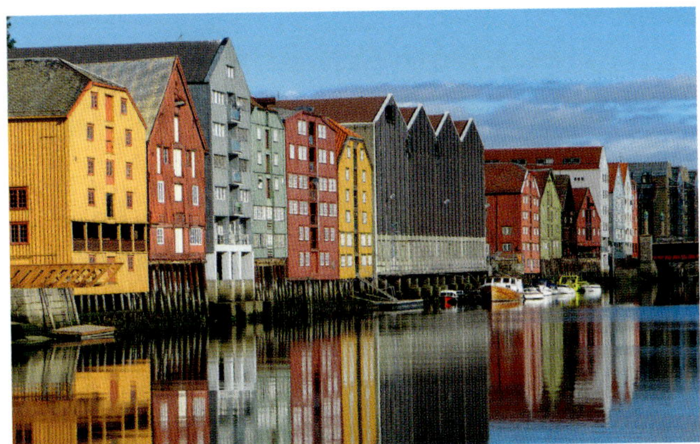

Trondheim, Norway: painted wood.

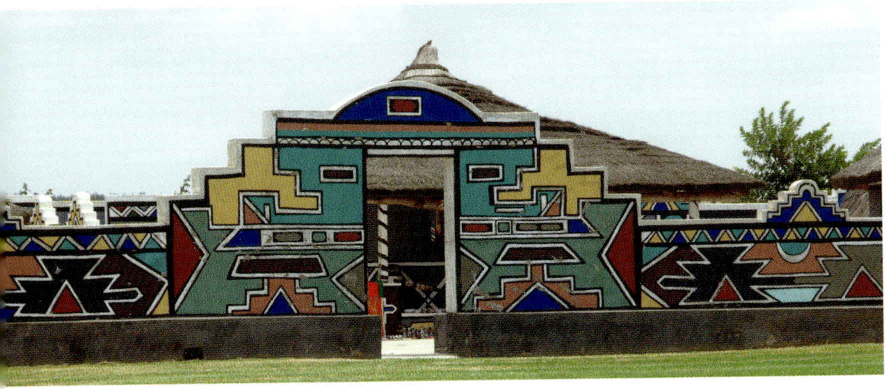

Traditional Ndebele architecture in South Africa: soil and cow dung.

46 GOETHE'S *THEORY OF COLOURS*

An influential book on color published in German in 1810 and translated into English by Charles Eastlake in 1840

- When renowned poet, playwright, novelist, and statesman Johann Wolfgang von Goethe (1749–1832) published *Zur Farbenlehre* (*Theory of Colours*), it brought a contextual wholeness to the field of color study.

- The book is a step-by-step exploration of color phenomena through an extensive sequence of detailed observations and experiments. Goethe wasn't seeking to measure, categorize, model, or explain color. As he writes, "The blue of the sky shows us the basic law of chromatics. Let us not seek for something behind the phenomena—they themselves are the theory."

- Goethe begins with the elusive colors that we experience physiologically, such as afterimages. He continues with the ephemeral colors that arise out of colorless conditions, like sunsets and prismatic colors. Then he investigates the permanent colors found in material substances, both inorganic and organic.

SEE ALSO Newton's *Opticks*

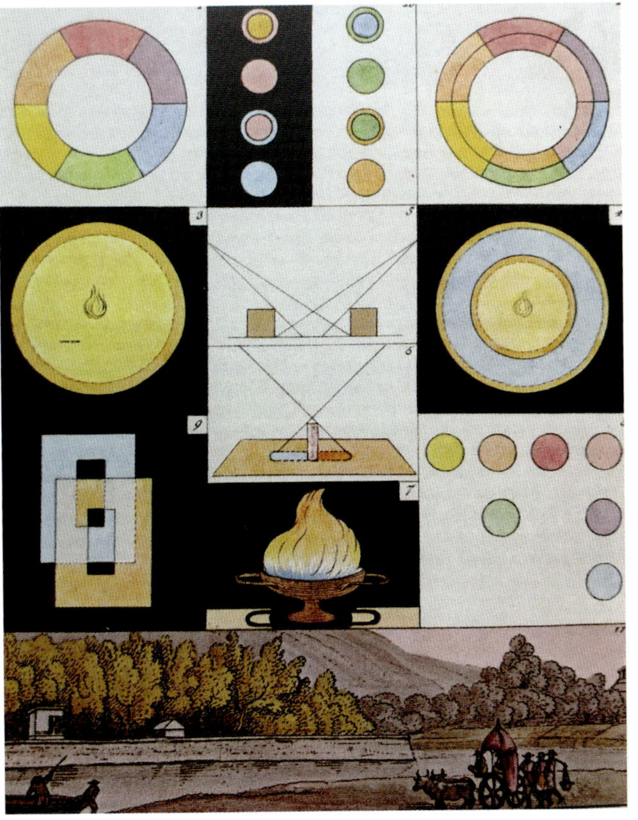

Illustrations of color phenomena from *Theory of Colours*.

47 GRADIENTS

The smooth blending of one color into another

- Found in plants, animals, flowers, and the sky, natural gradients can inspire artists and designers to integrate smooth blends of colors in their work.

- In fabric dyeing, and more recently hair dyeing, the gradient effect is called *ombre* (the French word for "shaded"). The popularity of the ombre effect comes and goes, but the process stays the same: dip dyeing for different lengths of time.

- In painting, there are many ways to mimic the effect. Wet-on-wet blending, dry brushing between two colors, and scumbling are just a few of the techniques used to smoothly blend colors from one to the other in paint.

- In computer graphics, the traditional gradient tools include linear and radial options. They are available in most design, drafting, and drawing programs and can be easily used to quickly create gradient backgrounds.

- More complex gradients can be constructed using software options such as the free-form gradient tool and the gradient mesh tool in Adobe Illustrator.

SEE ALSO Color Scales • Color Schemes • Flat Color

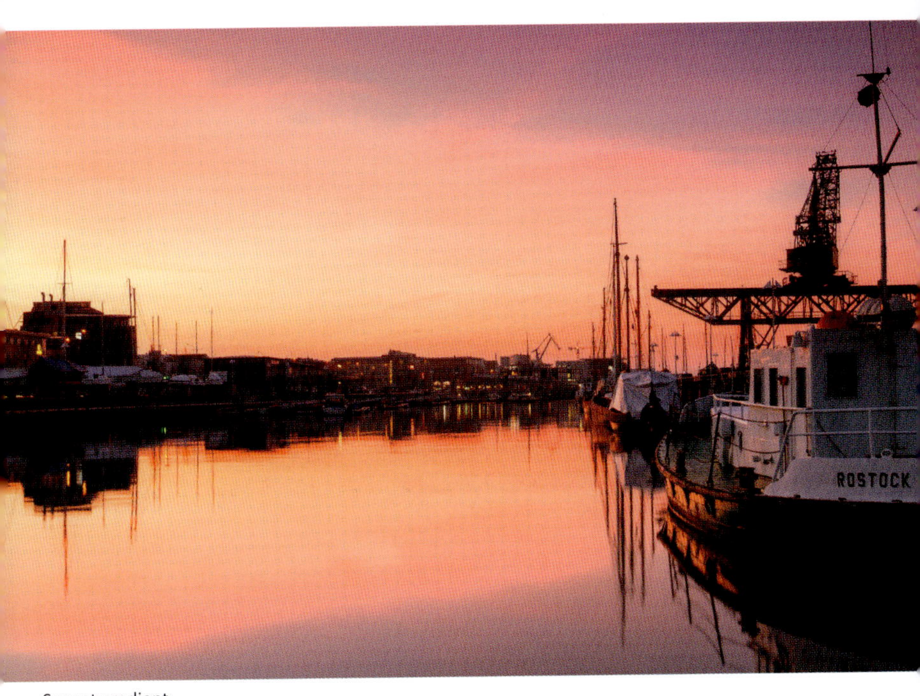

Sunset gradient.

48 GRISAILLE

A painting technique executed in shades of gray or other neutral color

- Grisaille is derived from *gris*, the French word for "gray." It is an oil painting technique, used particularly by Flemish artists in the fifteenth century, in which a composition is painted entirely in gray tones before successive layers of transparent glazes are applied on top. The underpainting provides a light and dark gradient to identify the relationships between forms.

- The technique has decreased in popularity in the modern era as new materials and techniques have been introduced, but the concept of identifying a gradient of light-to-dark continues to be a foundational tool for artists and designers.

SEE ALSO Black and White

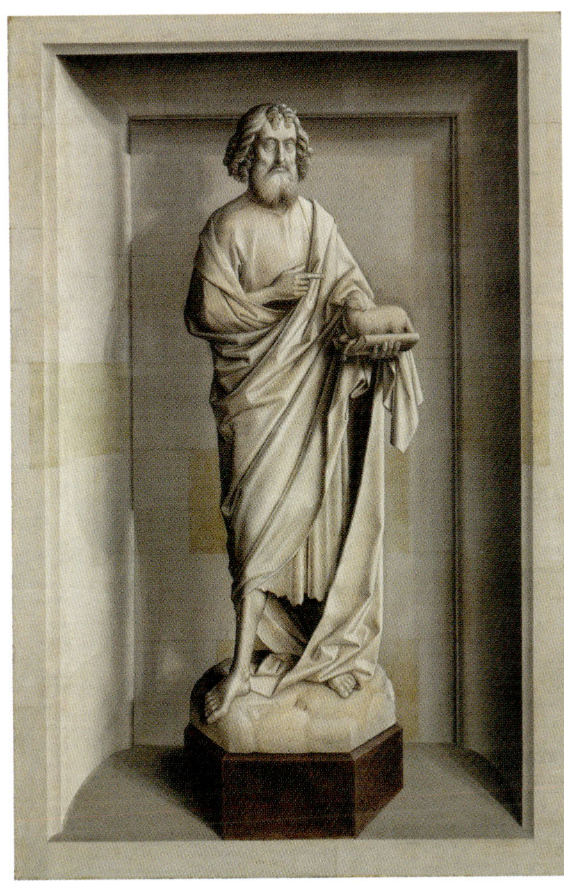

Saint John the Baptist (1475), Dieric Bouts. Because sculpture was more expensive than painting, the grisaille technique was often used to mimic sculptures.

49 HARMONY

The aesthetics of color relationships

- The aesthetics of color has been studied for centuries with many attempts to define rules that ensure harmony. Often described as a balance of separate but related parts, creating harmony is ultimately dependent on the decisions of the artist.

- Traditionally, most teaching about color harmony was focused on hue relationships. Simple geometric shapes were positioned in a circle and used to identify hue relationships, such as monochromatic, analogous, and complementary.

- Although hue combinations can be used to produce strong aesthetic responses, to achieve a harmonic combination of colors, lightness and chroma also need to be carefully considered. Furthermore, an aesthetic response to color combinations depends on several factors, including individual and cultural preferences, and the context in which the design or work of art is positioned.

- If related elements in art are considered harmonic, unrelated elements can be discordant. Discord can be used to provoke a deliberate challenge to the harmonic order.

Throughout history, attempts to quantify cultural and personal response to color have fallen short. What is harmonic for one person may be discordant for another.

SEE ALSO Balance • Color Schemes • Context • Hue Circle • Palettes

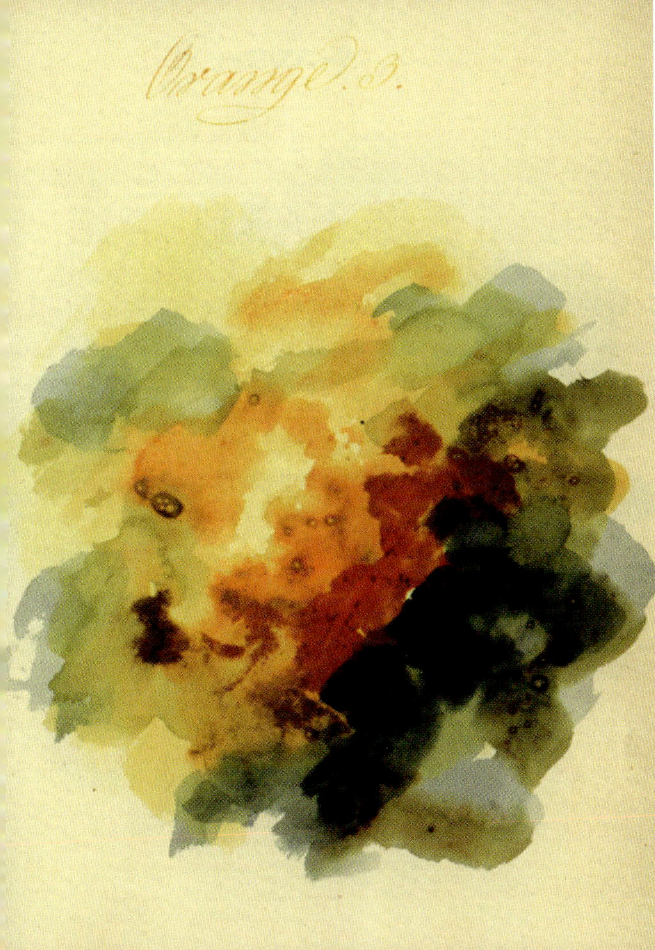

Illustration from *An Essay on Light and Shade, on Colours, and on Composition in General* (1805). Watercolor painting by Mary Gartside.

50 HUE ANGLE

The position of specific hues in polar relationship to a 360-degree hue circle

- There are two major types of hue-angle identifiers: those based on CIELAB, such as LCh, and those based on the RGB system for monitors, such as HSV and HSB. The hue angle represents all the colors on the hue plane at that position in color space.

LCh = Lightness, Chroma, Hue
HSV = Hue, Saturation, Value
HSB = Hue, Saturation, Brightness

	HSB/HSV	LCh
Monitor Red	0°	35°
Monitor Yellow	60°	90°
Monitor Green	120°	130°
Monitor Cyan	180°	195°
Monitor Blue	240°	300°
Monitor Magenta	300°	0°

Although it is often necessary to use Cartesian coordinates in specifying color, the advantage in becoming familiar with the polar coordinate system is that the attributes map onto our color vision experience much more closely than Cartesian coordinates such as L, a*, and b*.*

SEE ALSO CIE System • Hue Circle • RGB

CONSTANT HUE PLANE

Hue angles define vertical slices, known as constant hue planes, that are cut through a 3D color space. The example, at right, shows the circle of hue angles and red hue plane of the RAL system. In the red hue plane shown, the lightness increases from bottom to top and the chroma increases from left to right.

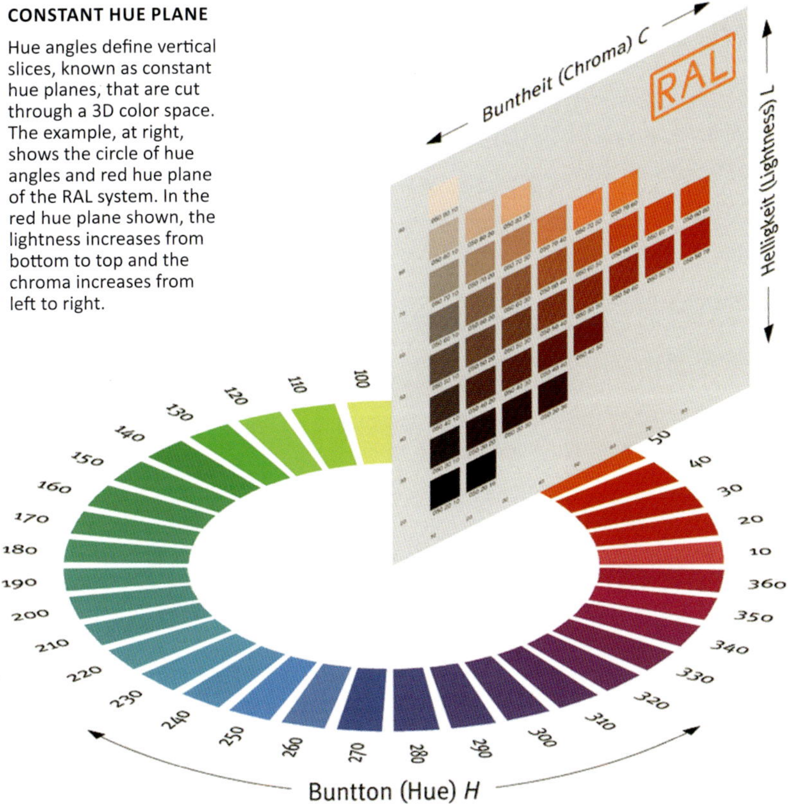

109

51 HUE CIRCLE

A circular arrangement that divides the spectrum into segments and illustrates the natural order of the spectral and nonspectral hues

- Isaac Newton is credited with introducing the hue circle, or hue wheel, around which he arranged seven hues—red, orange, yellow, green, blue, indigo, and violet.

- Since Newton's time, many different hue circles have been produced. Some purport to work as color mixing aids and begin with three so-called primary colors equally spaced around the circle. Simple six-hue wheels have a secondary color interspaced between each pair of primaries. Such wheels can be constructed starting with red, yellow, and blue (traditional artists' primaries); cyan, magenta, and yellow (optimal subtractive primaries); or red, green, and blue (additive primaries).

- Other hue circles, such as that in the HSB (hue-saturation-brightness) color space or the hue dimension of the CIELAB color space, do not begin with three primaries.

Despite many misconceptions, hue circles are useful for teaching students about the relationships between different hues.

SEE ALSO Hue Angle • Primary Colors • Three Dimensions of Color

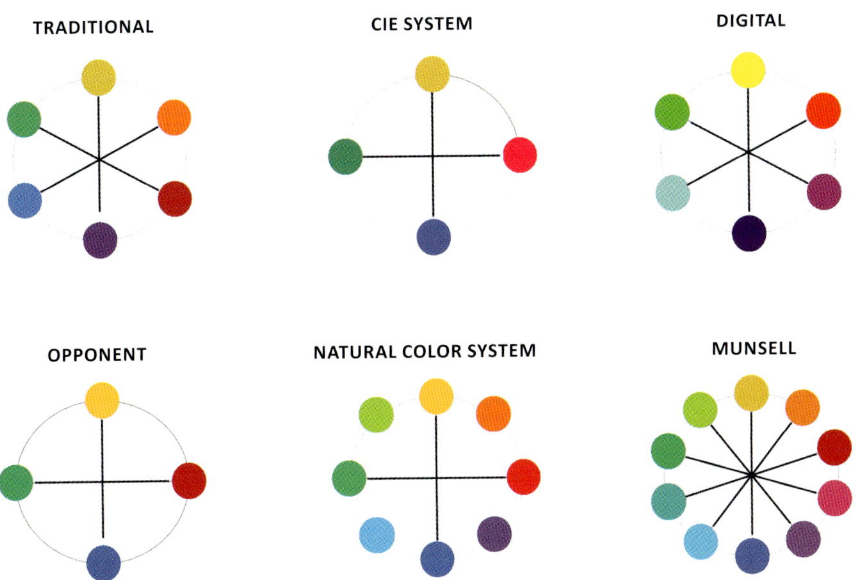

A comparison of hue circles shows the variations of hue placement in different color systems.

52 HUMAN VISUAL SYSTEM

The eye and the brain are fundamental for our perception of color

- The eye focuses light on the retina at the back of the eye, where light-sensitive cells known as rods and cones are located. At the front of the eye, the cornea and the lens provide focus. During normal levels of illumination, our color vision is mediated by three types of cone cells, which have maximal sensitivity at the short-, medium-, and long-wavelength parts of the spectrum, respectively.

- Cone signals activate retinal ganglion cells. The signals are combined and compared in the retina, providing the basis for visual phenomena such as contrast and opponency. The ganglion cells send signals to the brain's visual cortex, where cells respond strongly to visual stimuli.

- At very low levels of illumination, vision is mediated by the rods, and we see only in shades of gray. Brightness sensitivity shifts to shorter wavelengths; red objects appear darker, and blue objects appear lighter.

There is growing interest in the effect of color and light on health and well-being. Colors are, ultimately, a visual phenomenon.

SEE ALSO Blue Light • Limited Color Vision • Perception Triangle • Trichromacy

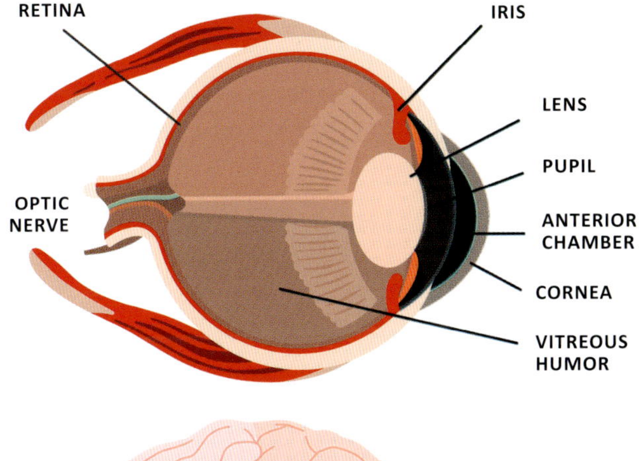

The retina of the eye contains light-sensitive cells that respond to light and send electrochemical signals to the brain.

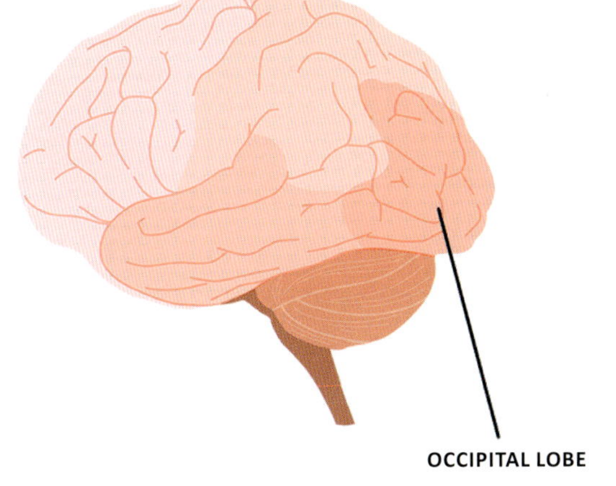

An important fact about the brain is that different areas are responsible for different functions. The visual cortex—which color and vision are associated with—is located in the occipital lobe.

53 IMPRESSIONISM

A nineteenth century art movement that aimed to replicate visual sensations of light and shadow in paintings characterized by rapid brushstrokes of color

- The term *Impressionism* derives from a Claude Monet painting titled *Impression, Sunrise*. Other notable Impressionists include Georges Seurat, Paul Cézanne, Camille Pissarro, and Pierre-Auguste Renoir.

- Based primarily in Paris, the Impressionist painters are known for works they produced in the open (*en plein*) air rather than in the studio, capitalizing on the recent invention of collapsible aluminum tubes. Renoir remarked that "without paint in tubes there would have been … nothing of what the journalists were later to call Impressionists."

- These innovative painters understood that one way to create the impression of a vivid chromatic hue was to juxtapose a hue next to its complementary hue. They rejected the method of mixing black or brown paint with a hue to create tonal variations and shadows. Instead, they employed small brushstrokes of complementary colors to construct chromatic shadows and establish a sense of depth in an image.

SEE ALSO Complementary Colors • Pointillism

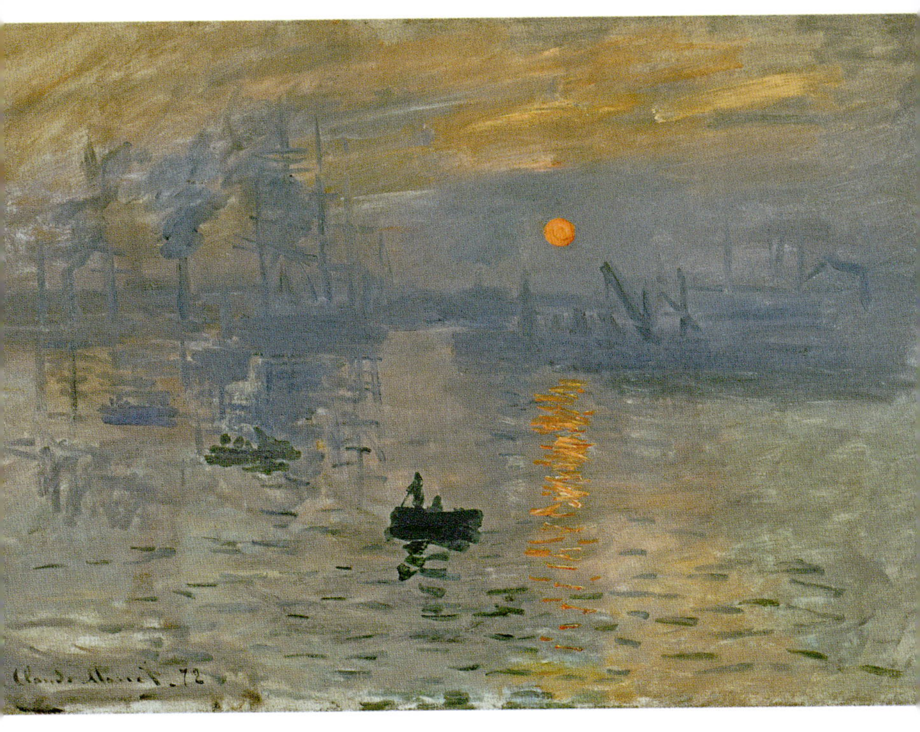

Impression, Sunrise (1872), by Claude Monet.

54 INFOGRAPHIC COLOR

The visual presentation of data in a pictorial or graphical format

- Color can be used to enhance the legibility of information in graphs, charts, diagrams, maps, and graphic illustrations, but the use of color must complement—not detract from—the main purpose of the overall design. Clarity is the primary purpose of using color in data visualization (DataViz) and information visualization (InfoViz).

- Accessibility of visual information and color meanings are key considerations in the design of infographics. For example, people with poor color discrimination or limited color vision may struggle to decipher poorly designed color combinations, which could render the intended information illegible. Also, insufficient consideration given to color associations (personal color preferences, cultural color biases and preferences) can make it more difficult for the viewer to assimilate the information embedded in the design.

When the design goal is to communicate clearly, use colors intentionally to strengthen the message.

SEE ALSO Accessibility • Color Scales • Flat Color • Gradients

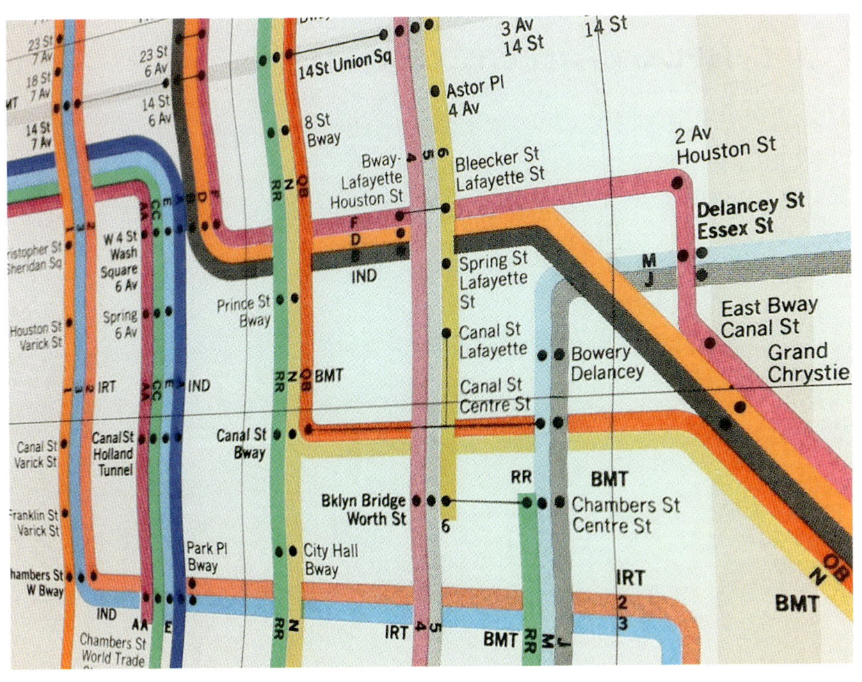

The classic NYC subway map (1972) by Massimo Vignelli is an example of using color to convey information.

55 INTERNATIONAL KLEIN BLUE

A brilliant blue paint developed, and later patented, by the French artist Yves Klein

- During the 1950s, Yves Klein, a leading member of the French artistic movement of nouveau réalisme, started to produce paintings that consisted of a single color. Public reaction to his exhibitions was underwhelming. Klein responded by entering a period where he painted using only the color blue.

- Klein's 1957 exhibition in Milan, *Proposte Monochrome, Epoca Blue*, featured eleven blue canvases that used ultramarine blue pigment suspended in a synthetic resin. Klein worked closely with a Parisian paint specialist to develop the brilliant paint color. It was a sensation and became known as International Klein Blue (IKB).

- Later Klein blurred the boundaries between painting and sculpture by using naked female models covered in his signature paint to impress their bodies onto sheets of paper.

- Today Klein's art can be found, among other places, in the Museum of Modern Art in New York and London's Tate Gallery.

SEE ALSO Brand Colors • Colorants • Emotion and Color • Symbolic Color

In 1957 Klein exhibited several canvasses that were painted entirely using the new International Klein Blue (IKB) pigment.

56 ITTEN'S *THE ART OF COLOR*

An influential book by Johannes Itten, a Swiss artist, designer, educator, and color theorist

- Johannes Itten (1888–1967) was one of the first teachers at the Bauhaus, where he taught from 1919 to 1923. He played a key role in developing the "preliminary course," which was designed to teach students the basic foundational concepts of composition, materials, and color.

- In 1961 Itten published *The Art of Color*, which promoted a twelve-hue color wheel based on perceptually "pure" red, yellow, and blue color primaries, ignoring many of the scientific developments of his contemporaries. Itten adhered to the view, held by most scientists until the mid-nineteenth century, that all object colors were mixtures of red, yellow, and blue.

- *The Art of Color* also promoted the idea of seven contrasts: hue, light and dark, cold and warm, complements, saturation, extension, and simultaneous contrast. Itten's approach permeated much subsequent color education and the body of knowledge known as traditional color theory.

SEE ALSO Albers's *Interaction of Color* • Bauhaus • Contrast • Traditional Color Theory

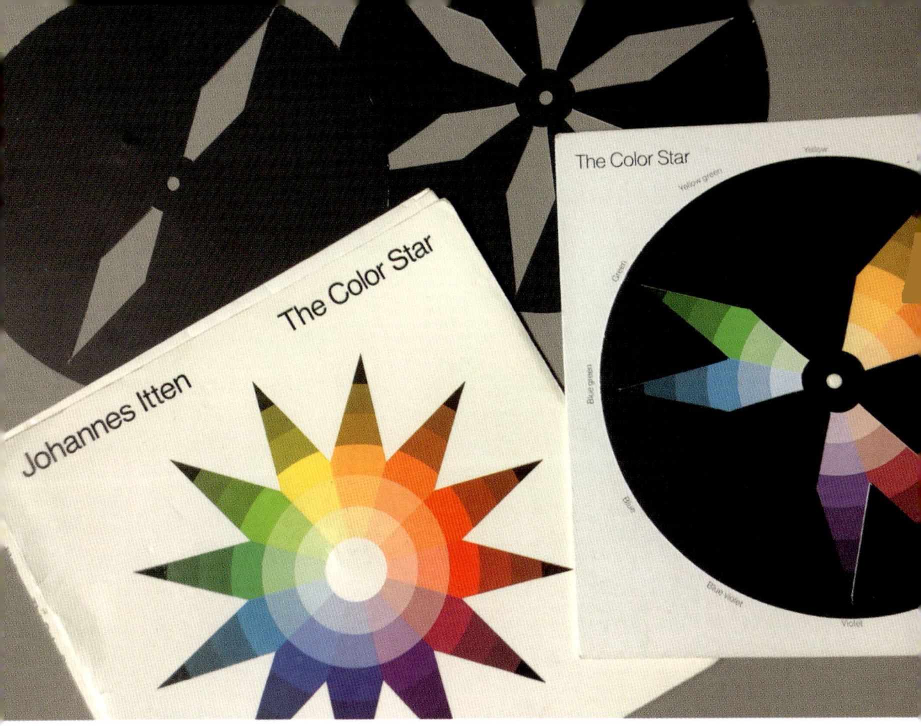

The Color Star (1986).

This color scheme tool is based on the traditional Red, Yellow, Blue color wheel from Itten's *The Art of Color*.

57 LED COLOR

A twentieth-century light source based on electricity passing through a semiconductor

- Early light-emitting diode (LED) lights were not very bright and limited to a few colors (first red, then yellow and orange). The first commercially available blue-emitting LED was based on silicon carbide. It was swiftly replaced with gallium nitride (c. 1990) by Shuji Nakamura and colleagues, who received the Nobel Prize in Physics in 2014.

- Early attempts to create white LEDs by mixing red, green, and blue light were only partially successful because the light produced had poor color rendering. Bright, efficient white LED light with good color-rendering properties was made possible by using a phosphor as a coating. Activated by the LED light, the phosphor produces light by fluorescence.

Thoughtful use of the extensive color capabilities of LED technology is recommended. The luminosity of LED colors, coupled with the affordability and efficiency of the technology, has the potential to saturate the world in artificial color.

SEE ALSO Color Temperature • Lighting

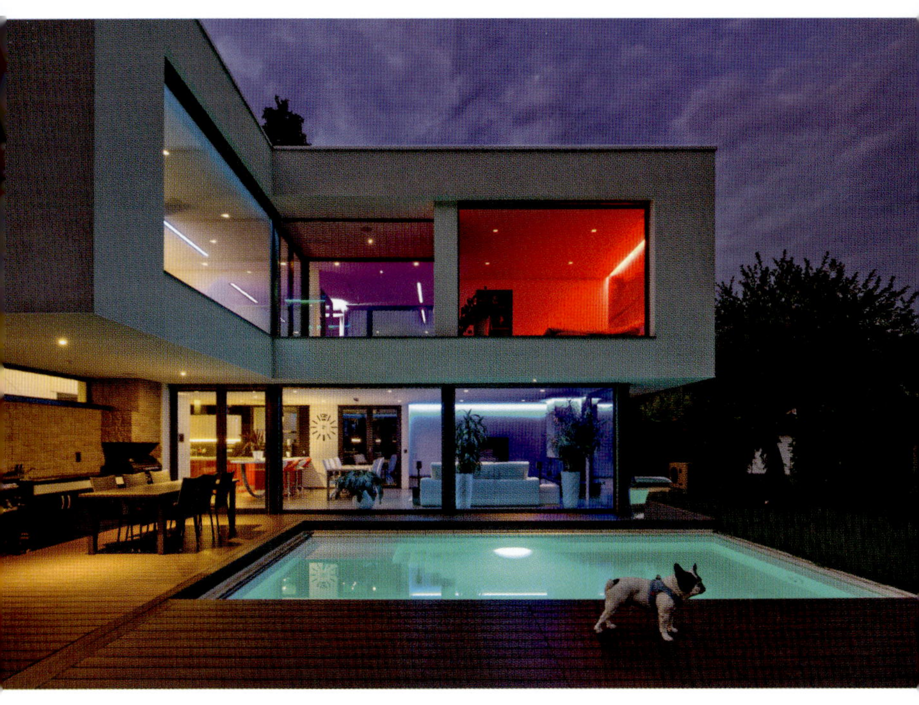

LEDs in private homes provide inexpensive and flexible lighting, but more research is needed on the impact of LED lighting on health and well-being at home and in the workplace.

58 LIGHTING

The deliberate use of light to achieve practical or aesthetic effects

- Humans have illuminated their environment for at least four hundred thousand years and possibly for one million years. For most of that time fire was used for both lighting and cooking. Candles have been used for a few thousand years, but efficient and effective manufactured lighting systems have only existed for the last few centuries.

- The use of gas lighting and incandescent light sources transformed our cities and led to the idea that "the city never sleeps."

- The color properties of light sources are determined by two different scales: Correlated color temperature (CCT) ranges from cool to warm. Color rendering index (CRI) rates how close the light source is to natural daylight and is used to quantify the effect of a light source on the color constancy of objects.

SEE ALSO Blue Light • Color Temperature • LED Color

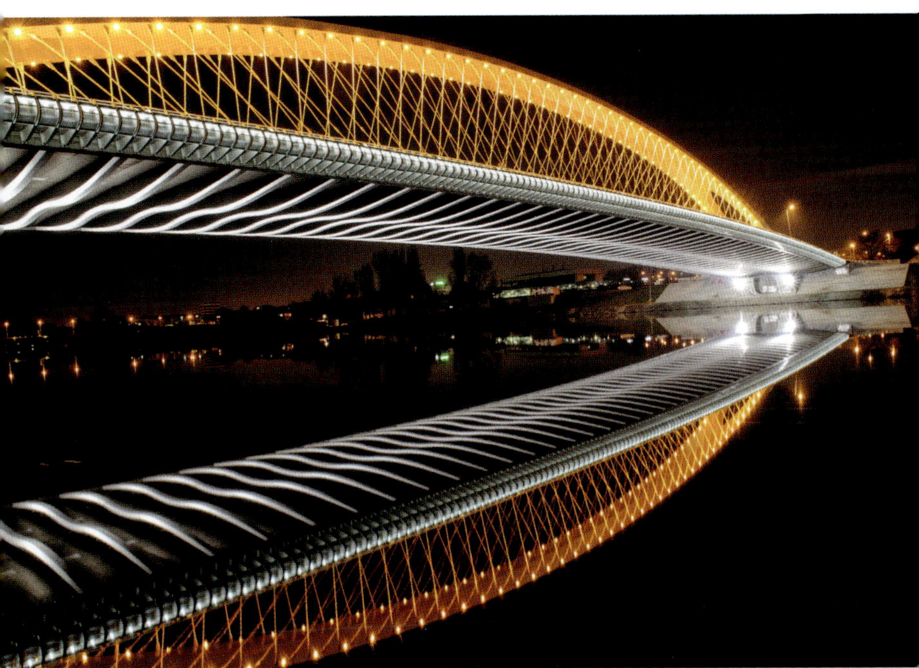

Dramatic use of light to generate an aesthetic effect: Troja Bridge, in Prague.

59 LIGHTNESS

Lightness is one of the three main attributes of color and describes the extent to which an object or light source appears to reflect or emit more or less light

- Lightness, also known as value, is a relative perception. Chromatically neutral objects that appear to emit a lot of light compared with other objects will likely appear white. Those that appear to emit little light compared with other objects will likely appear black.

- All colors can be assessed in terms of their lightness, an important consideration in design. For example, in terms of legibility, it is usually advisable that foreground (text) and background have a contrast in lightness because a contrast in hue alone can be very difficult to see or read.

The CIE defines lightness as "the brightness of an area judged relative to the brightness of an area that appears to be white or highly transmitting." Brightness is defined as "the amount of light perceived to be emitted or reflected by an area."

SEE ALSO Accessibility • Chroma • Three Dimensions of Color

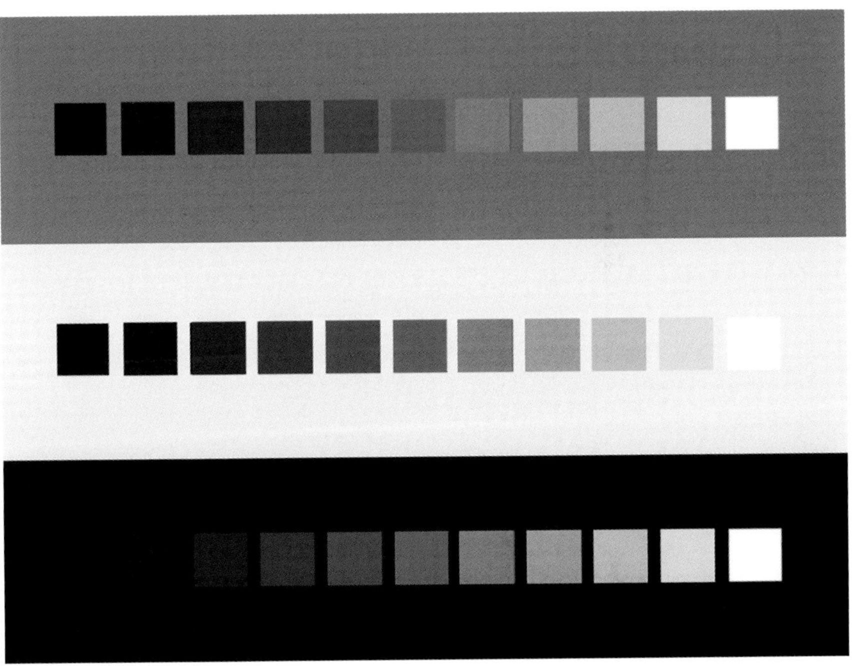

Effect of background on lightness perception and lightness scales.

The lightness scale in each case is identical and consists of an even scale of L= 0, 10, 20, 30, 40, 50, 60, 70, 80, 90, 100, but where is the biggest jump?

The phenomenon of "crispening" makes lightness intervals spanning the background lightness appear relatively large.

 LIMITED COLOR VISION

Physical condition of the retina leading to difficulty in discriminating between colors that other people can easily tell apart

- The term *color blindness* is a misnomer. *Color-deficient* is more accurate because most people with this condition can see different colors; they just have poor discrimination for certain parts of the color space (usually red and green).

- The difficulty distinguishing the amount of red or green in every color affects the perception of many colors. There are four types: protanomaly (red weakness), protanopia (red blindness), deuteranomaly (green weakness), and deuteranopia (green blindness).

- One widely used diagnostic test for color vision deficiencies, developed in 1917 by University of Tokyo professor Shinobu Ishihara, asks a person to read a number or trace a line in an image. In some cases, the number or line can be seen only by someone with normal color vision. In other cases, it can be seen only by someone with protanopia or deuteranopia.

- The Farnsworth-Munsell 100-hue test is designed with intentionally small steps between colors to measure a higher degree of color acuity.

SEE ALSO Accessibility • Human Visual System • Trichromacy

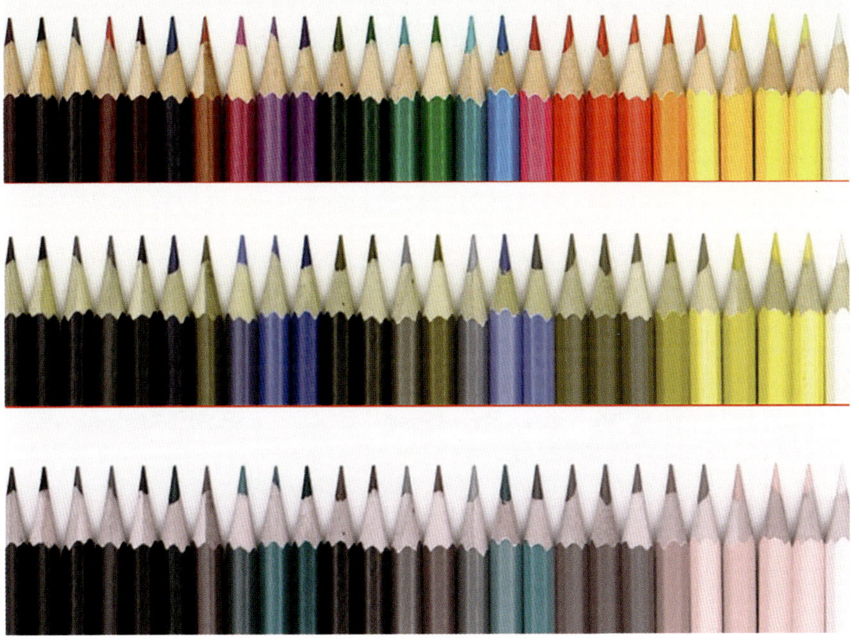

Simulations of how a set of colored pencils would look for someone with congenital color deficiency: normal vision (top), lack of long-wavelength cones (middle), and lack of short-wavelength cones (bottom).

61 LOCAL COLOR

The perceived color of an object under noon sunlight without the influence of lighting, surrounding colors, or viewing conditions

- Local color—also known as object, inherent, or nominal color—is one of the key factors that influences the perceived color of everything around us. Other factors that affect color include the lighting, viewing angle and distance, surrounding colors, surface textures, and shapes of the objects.

- One of the most enduring debates about color addresses the question: Is color a property of objects? The answer is complicated, but whether you believe that color is or is not a property of objects, all objects possess a "disposition" to absorb or reflect certain wavelengths of light, which are then channeled through our eyes and processed by our brains.

- Colorimetry instruments are used to measure object color by recording the light reflected by an object or sample without the influence of outside factors.

SEE ALSO Color Measurement • Human Visual System • Shadows

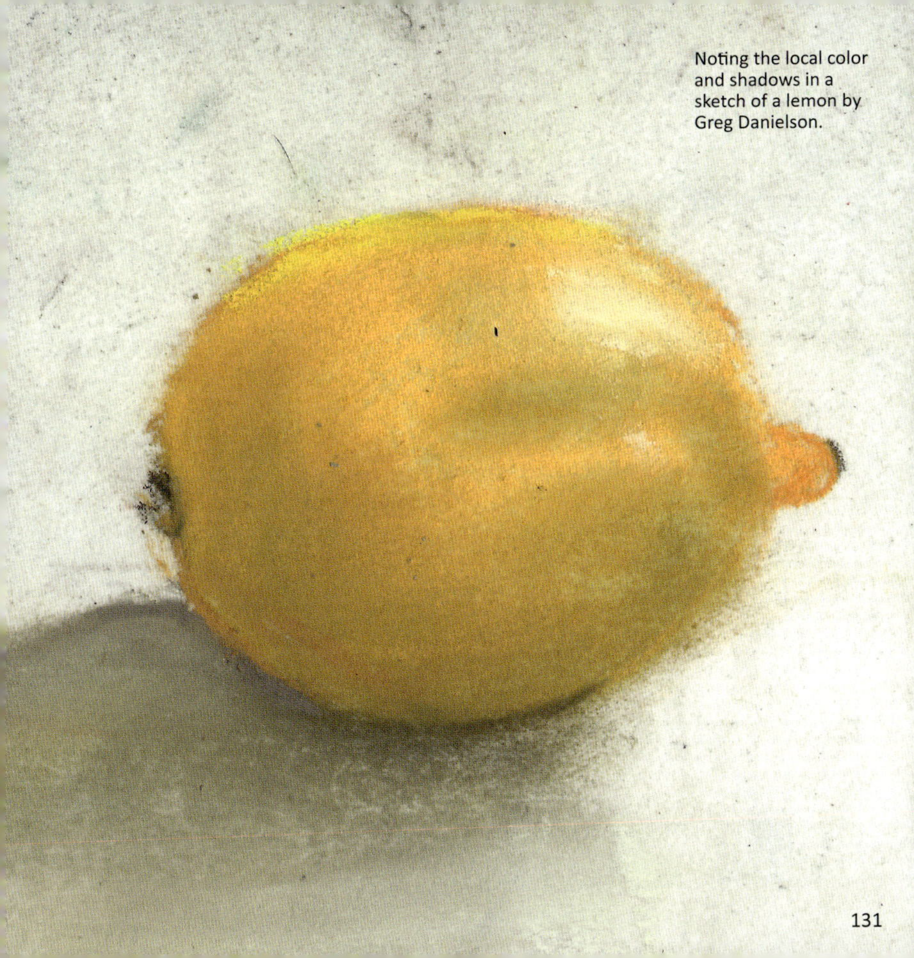

Noting the local color and shadows in a sketch of a lemon by Greg Danielson.

62 MAXWELL

Scottish scientist and mathematician who presented the first-ever color photograph

- James Clerk Maxwell (1831–1879) was a renowned scientist who made notable contributions in the fields of electromagnetic radiation, magnetism, and statistical thermodynamics. He was also a leading figure in the nineteenth-century development of our understanding of how color vision works.

- In the early nineteenth century, Thomas Young proposed that the human visual system operated using three channels. This became known as the trichromatic theory of color vision. We now know that the eye contains three classes of light-sensitive cells called cones. Maxwell developed mathematics and carried out experiments to provide evidence to support Young's proposal. Specifically, he showed that stimulation of the cones could be achieved using an additive mixture of three monochromatic lights, thus inventing the field of colorimetry upon which the current CIE system is based.

- The gamut of colors that can be achieved by additively mixing three primaries is a triangle when shown in two dimensions. Maxwell was the first to show this triangular arrangement, and these triangular gamuts are known as Maxwell triangles.

SEE ALSO CIE System • Partitive Mixture • RGB

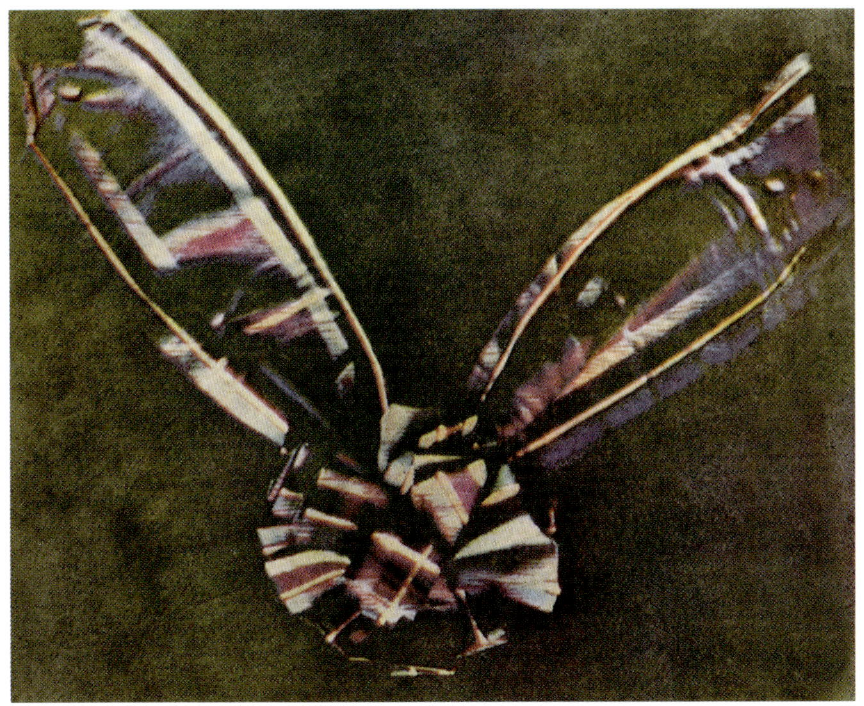

In 1861, James Clerk Maxwell presented the world's first color photograph at the Royal Institution. The photograph was captured by Thomas Sutton, who took three images of a Scottish tartan through red, green, and blue filters. He then superimposed these three images using a projection system to create a color image, establishing the principles through which color imaging would later develop.

63 METAMERISM

Colors that match under one lighting condition can appear to not match under a different lighting condition

- The human visual system's response to a color stimulus is limited to the response of the light-sensitive receptors in the eye called cones. The light that reaches the eye when we look at objects is a property of both the spectral distribution of the illumination and the spectral reflectance (or transmission) properties of the object.

- Illuminant metamerism occurs when two spectrally dissimilar objects appear to be the same color when viewed under one light source but fail to match under a second light source.

- Other types of metamerism include geometric (two objects match when viewed from one angle but not from a second angle), size (two objects match when viewed from one distance but not from a different distance), and observer (two objects match when viewed by one observer but not when viewed by a second observer).

- Metamerism requires the objects to be spectrally dissimilar. If two objects have identical reflectance spectra, they will likely be a match to an observer under all conditions.

SEE ALSO Color Temperature • Human Visual System • Lighting

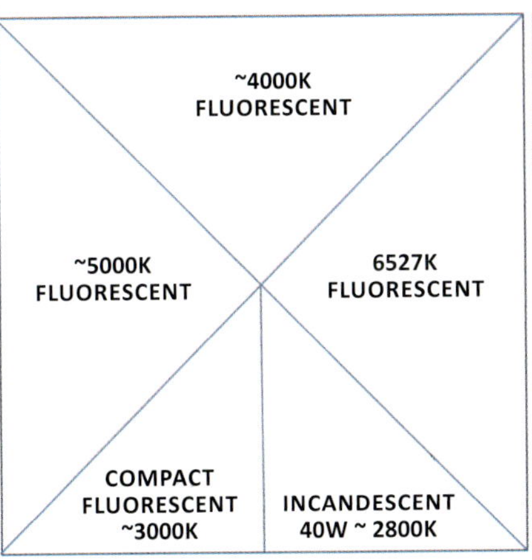

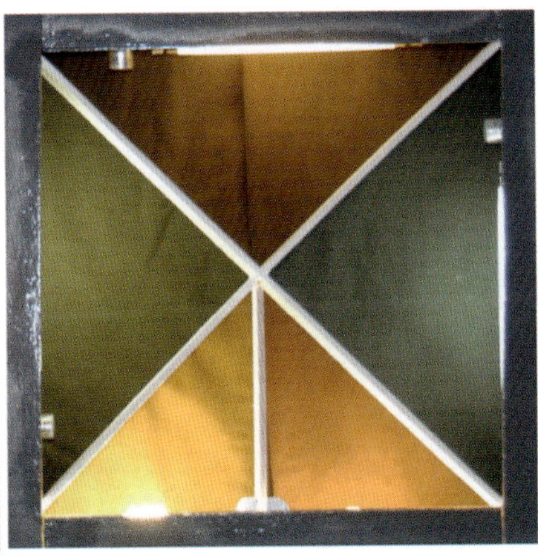

A booth used at the Color Science and Imaging laboratory, North Carolina State University, for testing the appearance of the same fabric under different lighting conditions can predict the effects of metamerism.

64 MONOCHROMATIC

A color scheme that features variations of a single hue

- A monochromatic color scheme, also known as harmony of dominant hue, is one where the component colors have the same hue but vary in lightness and chroma.

- Art that contains a single hue was sometimes produced by expressionist artists; for example, in Picasso's blue period he produced paintings that contained only blue or blue-green.

- Sometimes there is a fine distinction between a strictly monochromatic color scheme and one that is analogous, where the colors are similar but not identical in hue.

- A monochromatic wash is sometimes used in movies, or in advertisements for movies, to communicate a particular emotion or feel for a scene. In graphic design, a monochromatic color scheme can be both visually and cost-effective. In science, the term *monochromatic* sometimes has a slightly different meaning; it refers to a single-wavelength light source.

SEE ALSO Color Schemes • International Klein Blue

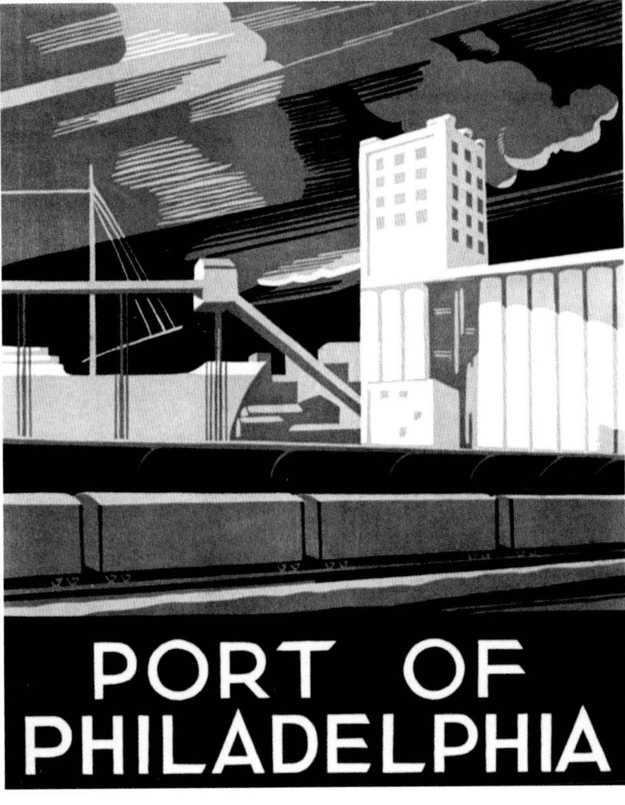

This WPA poster uses a simple monochromatic scheme with a single blue hue shifting to black and to white.

MUNSELL SYSTEM

A color model and specification system created by artist and art educator Albert Munsell in the early 1900s

- Munsell based his system on color perception rather than paint mixing. It has five principal hues (red, yellow, green, blue, and purple) and three attributes, which he called dimensions (hue, value, and chroma).

- To measure and describe color variations, Munsell invented a photometer for determining value, equivalent to lightness. To determine chroma, he used Maxwell disks to compare the visual color strength of colored papers. These measurements resulted in the system's distinctive asymmetrical arrangement of swatches around the central neutral axis.

- The system's main purpose is numerical color communication. For example, the Munsell notation 5R 5/12 is a sample with a Munsell hue of middle red, a middle value of 5, and a moderately strong chroma of 12.

- The Munsell system is the basis for CIELAB and remains useful for educating students about the perceptual attributes of color.

SEE ALSO Color Order Systems • Natural Color System • Three Dimensions of Color

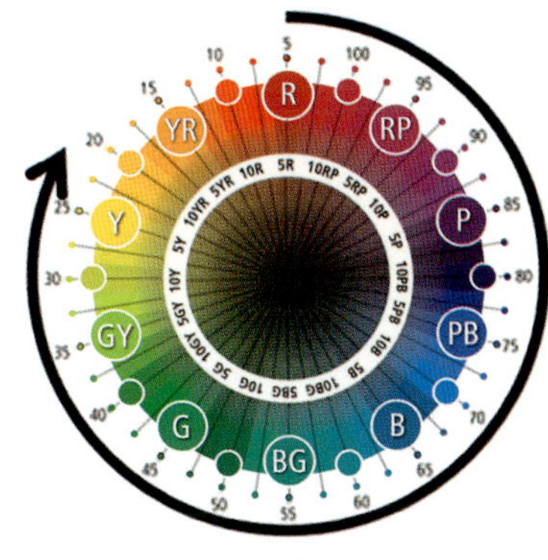

HUE

The system is based on perceptually even spacing in three dimensions that Munsell called hue, value (lightness), and chroma. Colors can shift in three directions: around the hue circle, up and down in lightness/value, and in and out from the central gray axis.

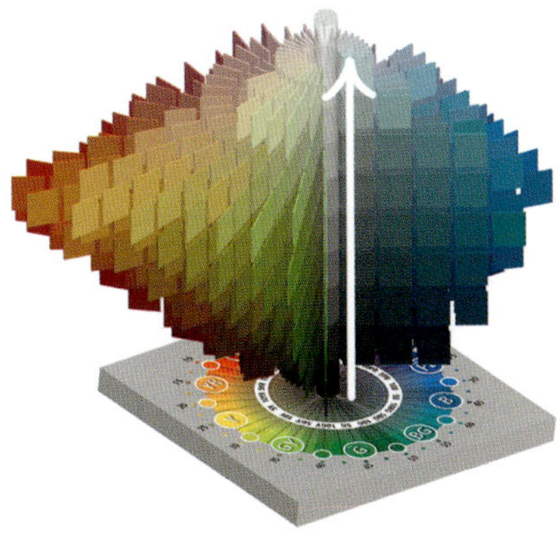

VALUE

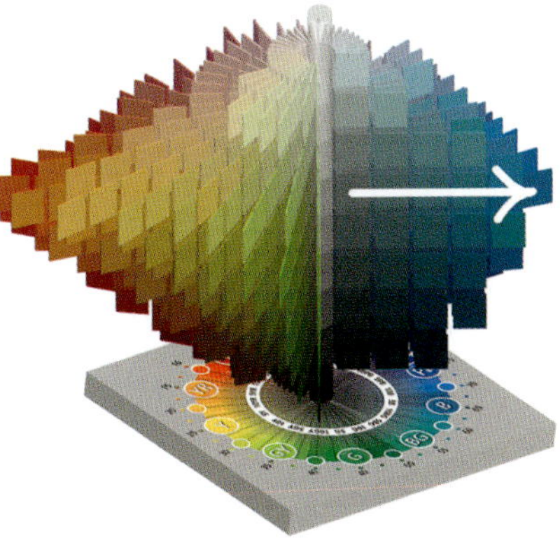

CHROMA

66 NATURAL COLOR SYSTEM

A proprietary tool for color communication and color description developed in Sweden in the 1960s

- The NCS's perceptual color model is based on the color opponency hypothesis of color vision that was first postulated by Ewald Hering in 1892 and was developed at the Swedish Colour Centre Foundation in the 1960s. The basic concept is that all color perceptions can be defined in terms of their similarity to six elementary color percepts that form three pairs: white/black, green/red, and yellow/blue. A shocking pink, for example, would be defined by its visual similarity to red, blue, and black.

- NCS notation uses three values to define every color perception: degree of blackness (S), degree of chromaticness (C), and hue. In terms of hue, every color can be described by its similarity to two terms. For example, a color can be red or blue or red-blue, but it cannot be red-green because red and green are opponent colors in the system. The NCS is particularly popular in architecture and interior design applications.

SEE ALSO Character Zones • Munsell System • Unique Hues

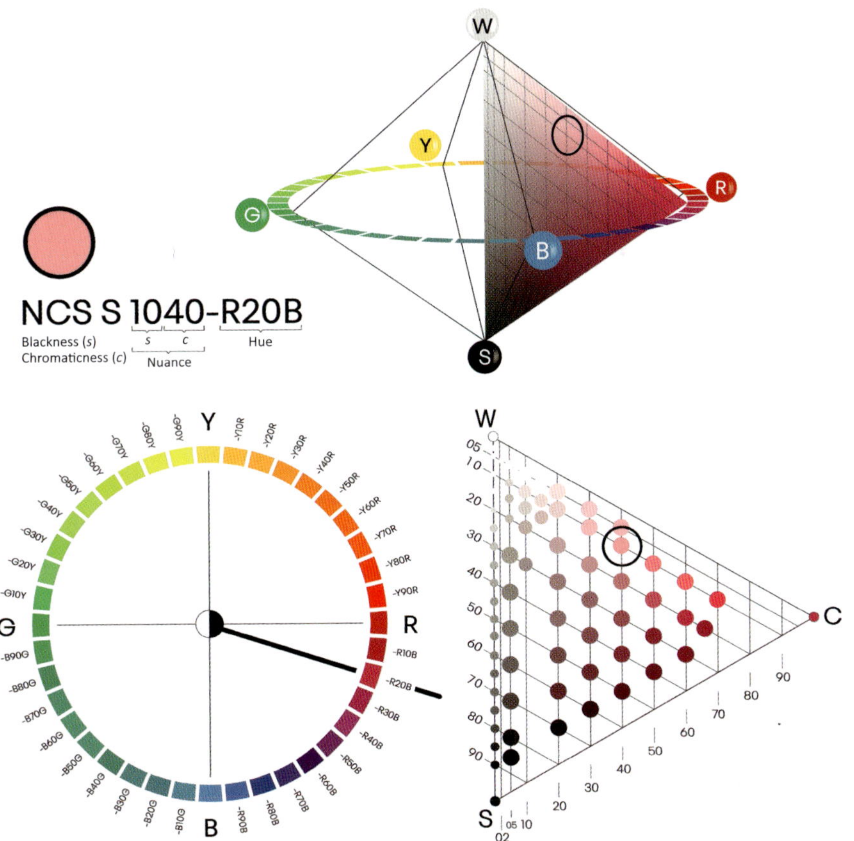

W
Y
R
G
B
S
NCS S 1040-R20B
Blackness (s)
Chromaticness (c)
s
c
Nuance
Hue
Y
-G90Y
-G80Y
-G70Y
-G60Y
-G50Y
-G40Y
-G30Y
-G20Y
-G10Y
G
-B90G
-B80G
-B70G
-B60G
-B50G
-B40G
-B30G
-B20G
-B10G
B
-Y10R
-Y20R
-Y30R
-Y40R
-Y50R
-Y60R
-Y70R
-Y80R
-Y90R
R
-R10B
-R20B
-R30B
-R40B
-R50B
-R60B
-R70B
-R80B
-R90B
W
C
S
05
10
20
30
40
50
60
70
80
90
02
05 10
20
30
40
50
60
70
80
90

67 NATURE'S LIGHT

Sunlight and moonlight illuminating the natural world

- The world around us is illuminated by the sun and the moon. Nature's light shifts in color over the course of the day in different weather conditions, and from season to season due to the angle at which light enters the atmosphere and atmospheric conditions.

- The CIE defines light as electromagnetic radiation that is visible, and this is generally taken to be the wavelength range of 360 nm to 780 nm. However, the precise limits of visibility depend on the viewing conditions, the intensity of the radiation, and the individual.

- Light sources can be defined by their spectral power distribution. Natural daylight has a broad, even power distribution, whereas an incandescent light bulb has a distribution that increases markedly toward the longer (redder) wavelengths.

- The color temperature of natural daylight can range from the warm light of 1900 Kelvin at sunrise and sunset to a cool 6000K at noon.

SEE ALSO CIE System • Color Temperature • Electromagnetic Spectrum • Newton's *Opticks* • Rayleigh Scattering

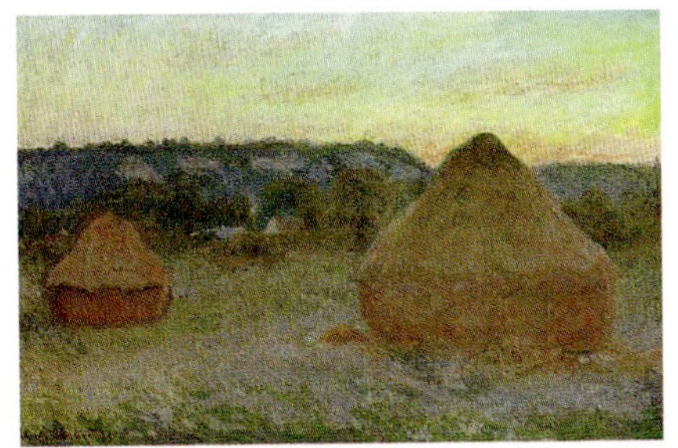
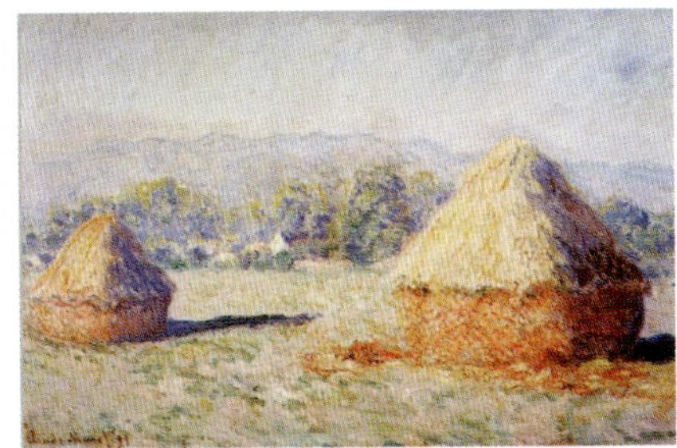
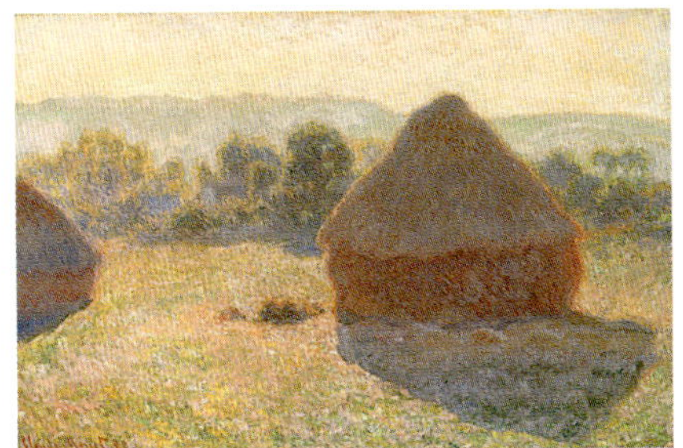
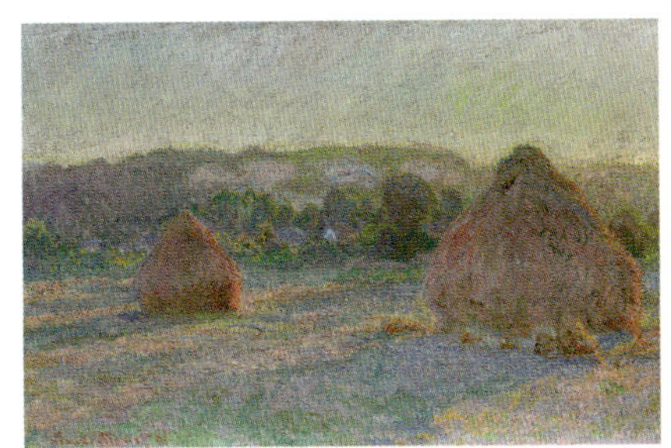

Haystack paintings at different times of the day by Monet.

143

Low-chroma colors that appear almost gray but have underlying hues

- Sometimes called chromatic grays or chromatic neutrals, near-neutral colors are muted colors located close to the neutral axis in 3D color space. The underlying hue, or undertone, determines their position on the hue circle.

- Due to their low chroma, the appearance of near neutrals can be strongly affected by lighting and surrounding colors. Side-by-side comparison under the same lighting conditions is necessary to establish the underlying hue.

- Near-neutral colors are ubiquitous in interior design and fashion design.

SEE ALSO Lightness • Three Dimensions of Color • Undertone

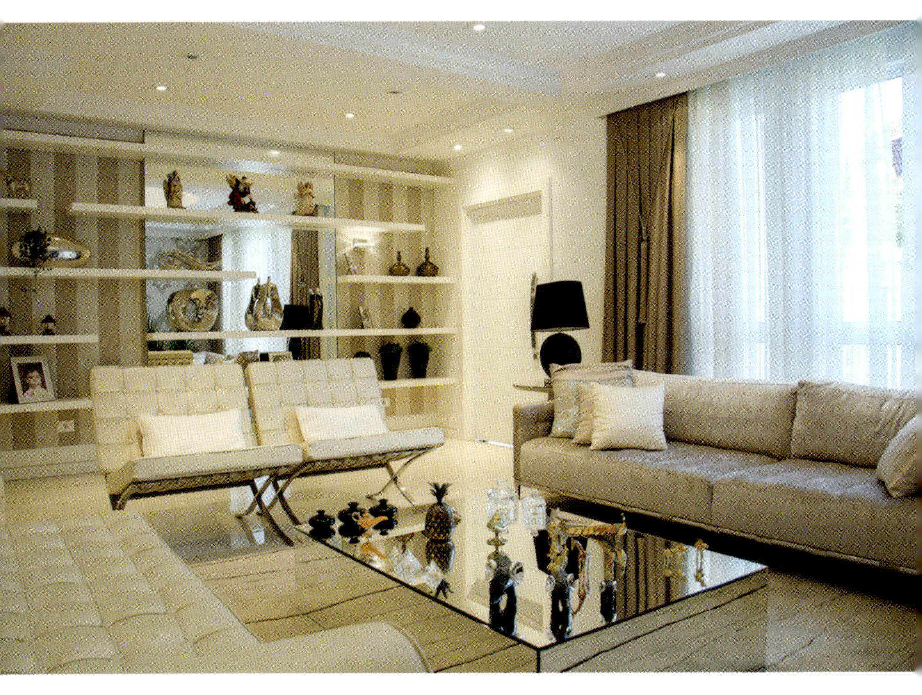

Near neutrals featured in the interior design of a living room.

69 NEWTON'S *OPTICKS*

Isaac Newton published *Opticks* in 1704 and profoundly changed the way we think about color

- Isaac Newton (1643–1747) is famous for passing white light through a glass prism and noting that the white light separated into a band of different colors, negating the earlier belief that white light became colored as it traveled through the prism because it picked up impurities from the glass itself.

- The realization that when different-colored lights overlapped, they generated light of a different color—which we now know as additive mixing—transformed how Newton's contemporaries thought about color.

- Newton used the term *refrangibility* to describe how some colored light changed direction more than other colors when it entered the prism. We now know that it is due to the wavelength of light. He also understood that hue perception is circular and that some hues, such as purple and magenta, cannot be observed as single wavelengths.

- Newton named the seven colors that can be observed in the visible spectrum: red, orange, yellow, green, blue, indigo, and violet.

SEE ALSO Additive Mixture • Electromagnetic Spectrum • Spectral Hues

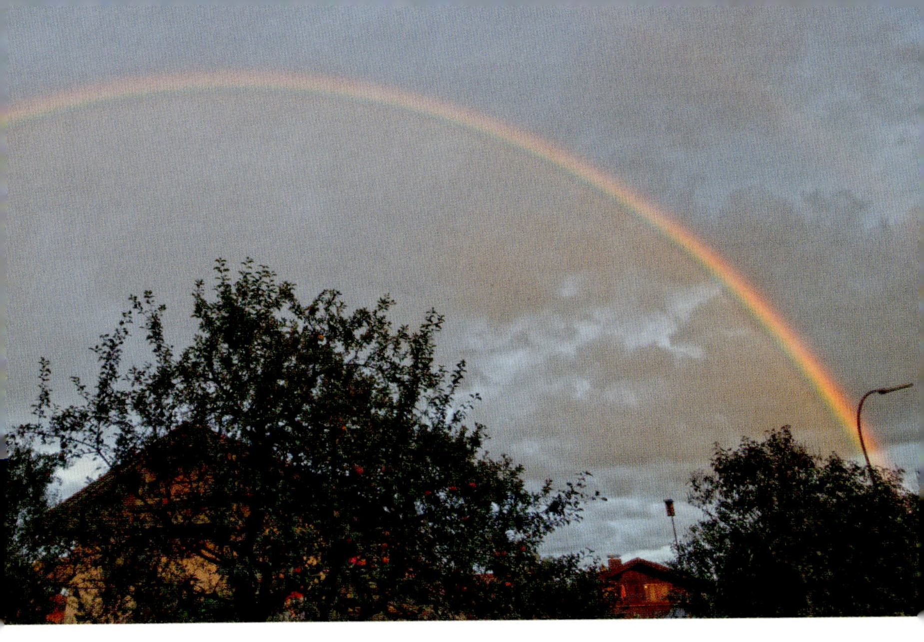

The same effect that Newton observed with a glass prism can be seen in the rainbow. A rainbow forms because of diffraction of light by water droplets in the atmosphere. The order of the rainbow colors is often taught using the seven colors of Newton's color wheel.

70 OP ART

Abstract art characterized by geometric patterns creating optical illusions

- Op ("optical") artists of the 1950s and 1960s explored the phenomena of visual perception in abstract paintings that intentionally trick the eye by creating the illusion of motion and 3D space using only line and color.

- Op art was the focus of *The Responsive Eye* exhibit at Museum of Modern Art in 1965, which featured paintings and sculptures by artists such as Victor Vasarely, Richard Anuszkiewicz, Bridget Riley, Frank Stella, Ellsworth Kelly, Kenneth Noland, and Josef Albers.

- In the exhibition catalog, curator William C. Seitz wrote, "The eye responds most directly when nonessentials such as freely modulated shape and tone, brush gestures and impasto are absent. These means muffle and distort the purely perceptual effect of lines, areas, and colors. ... Every work chosen for this exhibition, therefore, is entirely abstract."

Although the pinnacle of the movement was in the 1960s, the abstraction and optical effects of op art continue to influence artists and designers.

SEE ALSO Advancing and Receding • Albers's *Interaction of Color* • Bauhaus • Flat Color

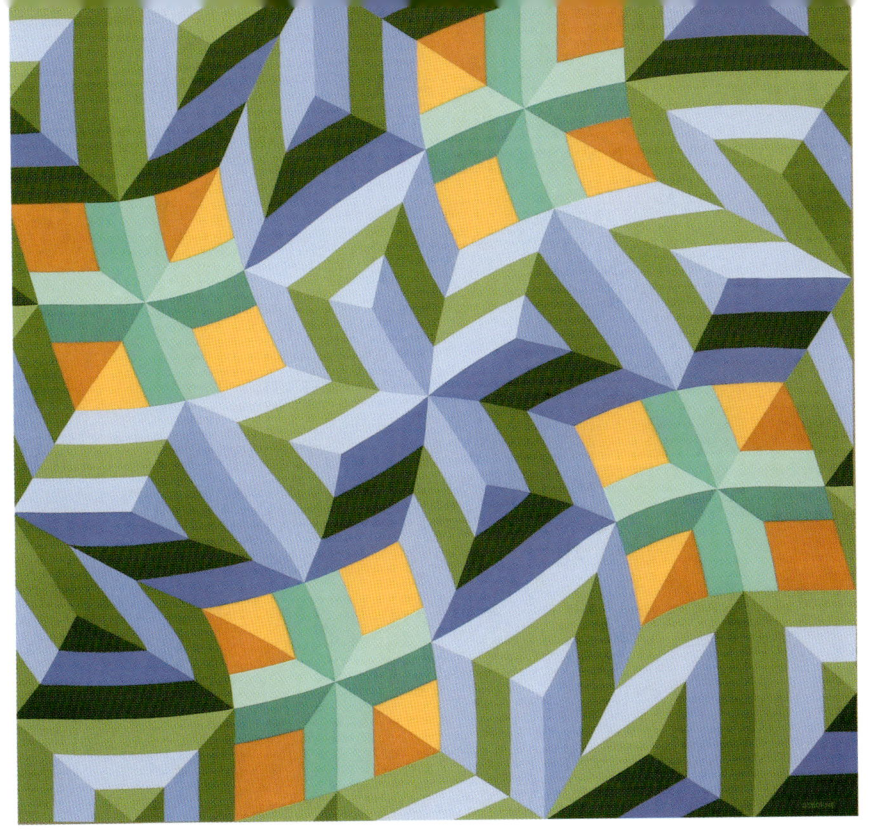

Crossways IX (2015–2020), by Roy Osborne.

71 PALETTES

The range of colors used by an artist or designer for a project

- In the process of creating a work of art or design, artists and designers select a set of colors that determines the appearance and overall gestalt of the work. The palette refers to all the colors in the set, which can include vivid hues, chromatic neutrals, and achromatic colors. Some colors may be more dominant, while others may be used as accents.

- In physical media such as paints, inks, and dyes, the range of colors available is dependent on the selection of colorants selected for the palette.

- In digital media, the palette is more extensive due to the large gamut possible in display technologies.

- In environmental design, palettes are based on the selection of materials and include the colors of natural and applied finishes.

Artists and designers often develop a signature palette that makes their work distinct and easily recognizable in any medium.

SEE ALSO Color Schemes • Colorants • Colorways • Gamuts

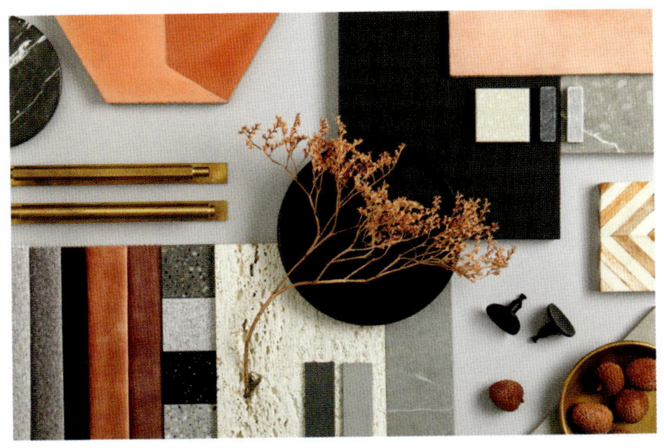

Interiors palette.

A limited palette for interiors that combines materials in natural and applied colors.

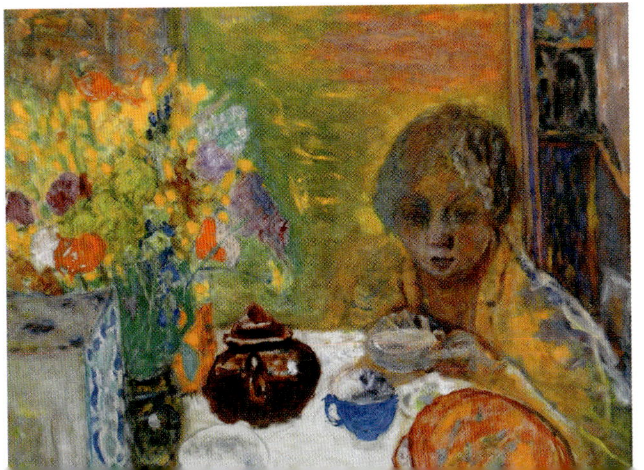

Full palette.

Le Dejeuner (1932), by Pierre Bonnard.

72 PANTONE™

Proprietary color communication tools designed for the accurate specification and communication of color

- The Pantone company was formed in 1962 by Lawrence Herbert and is primarily known for its color communication tools. These are available in various forms including books and individual swatches, but typically consist of a fan deck in which each page contains samples that are similar in hue. These decks are produced to a high degree of reproducibility so that designers can identify a color and communicate the specific Pantone ID to a client with an identical fan deck.

- Originally started as a printer ink company, Pantone now intentionally markets to designers. The Pantone Color of the Year announcements, started in 2000, lead the way in trendsetting colors for branding, marketing, and creative industries around the world.

The provision of a printing ink recipe in the original Pantone system has contributed to the widespread use of Pantone as a color communication and specification system in the printing and graphic arts industries.

SEE ALSO CMYK • Color Management

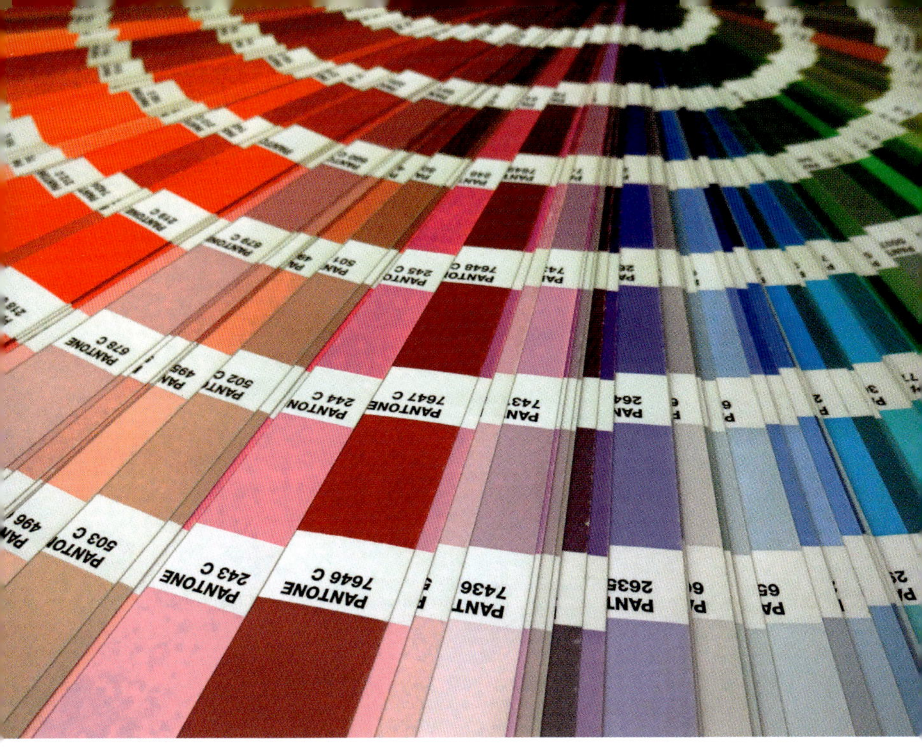

An example of a
Pantone fan deck
showing a range of
different colors.

73 PARTITIVE MIXTURE

The perception of color mixture that occurs due to spatial or temporal averaging of colors

- In addition to the additive mixture of light and the subtractive mixture of paints, inks, and dyes, there is a third type of color mixture known as partitive, optical, or additive averaging.

- The pointillist painters explored the effects of partitive mixture using small strokes of paint. The farther away you stand, the more the distinct colors blend together. This technique is an example of spatial averaging.

- Weaving is another example of spatial averaging. The distance required for the averaging of the colors depends on the fineness of the threads. The thinner the threads, the more quickly the colors optically mix.

- Temporal averaging is best demonstrated by the optical mixtures created by spinning disks. The most famous were those used by Maxwell in his explorations of color, where the slit in the circle of colored paper allowed for easy adjustment of the proportions.

Partitive mixture results in averaging the attributes of color.

SEE ALSO CMYK • Color Management • Maxwell • Pointillism • RGB

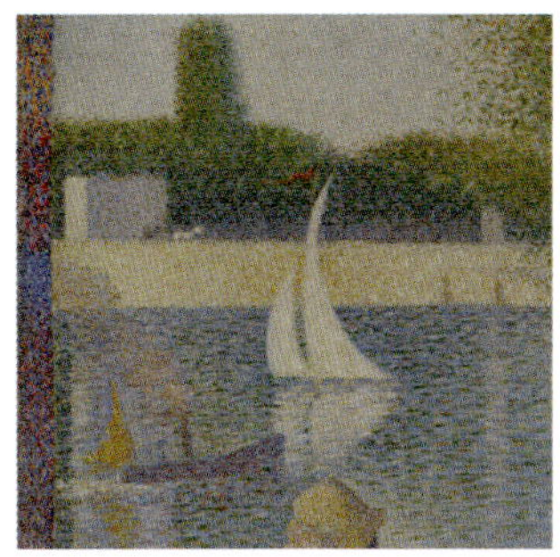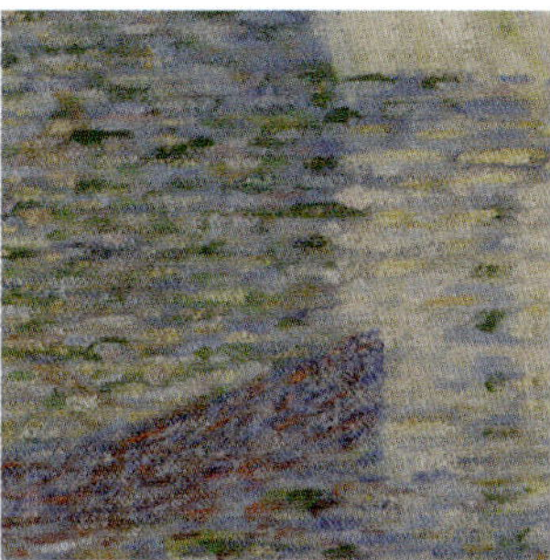

A Sunday on La Grande Jatte (1884), by Georges Seurat. Detail of a section in the upper left of the painting with an even finer detail showing the paint strokes.

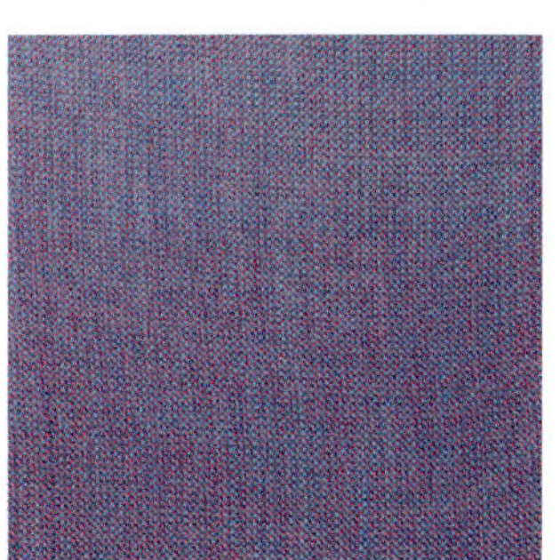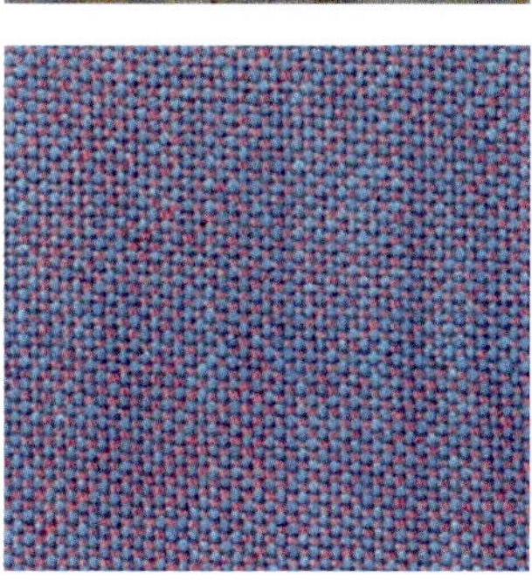

In plain weave, the even distribution of the two colors of the warp and weft optically blend together and appear to be a single solid color with only a small amount of variation.

74 PERCEPTION TRIANGLE

The relationship between the light source, the object, and the observer in the perception of color

- Generally, we see objects as being colored because of the brain's response to light that is reflected or transmitted by objects. The perception triangle—which indicates that light, object, and observer are all important—reveals the insight that color is not simply a property of an object, although we often speak as if it is. For example, we might say that the bird is red whereas it would be more accurate to say that it looks red.

- It is firmly established that the color appearance of an object often changes depending on the quality and quantity of a light source. An object's apparent color may also depend on the properties of the observer (e.g., when someone has limited color vision).

While the perception triangle somewhat oversimplifies the complexity of color perception, it is a good starting point when teaching about color. Whereas our everyday experience of color would often suggest that it is simply the property of an object, we know that it depends on the lighting and the observer, in addition to many other factors including context effects such as the surrounding colors.

SEE ALSO Bezold Effect • Context • Electromagnetic Spectrum • Human Visual System • Nature's Light • Simultaneous Contrast

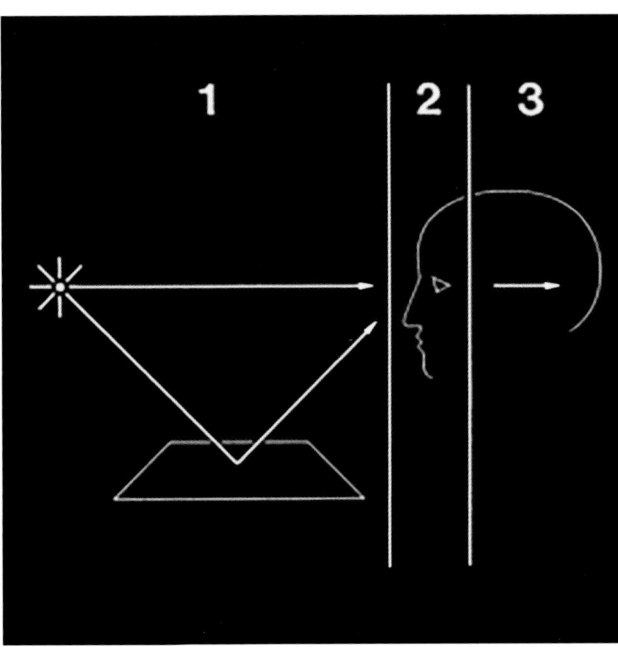

"When we see colors, processes are involved in this sensory experience which take place in three different areas, one after the other:

1-Physical events outside the human body (light)

2-Reaction of the visual organs to light stimulus

3-Occurrence of the visual experience in the brain."

Text and graphic by Moritz Zwimpfer.

75 **PERMANENCE**

The ability of colorants to stay colorfast when exposed to light and heat

- Most manufactured materials are colored due to the application of colorants that selectively absorb light. Over time, exposure to heat or light can cause the colorant molecules to break down, destroying the chromophore—that part of the molecule that absorbs light. This can lead to pigments or dyes that are said to be "fugitive," meaning they will fade over time.

- When choosing colorants for a particular application, the selection of permanent versions is often an important consideration. For example, colorants applied to clothing need to remain in the fabric when washed in hot water. Colorants for products or artwork that are used or displayed outside need to have high light fastness.

- Manufacturers now label pigments with a light fastness rating. The two main measurement scales are the American Society for Testing and Materials (ASTM) scale and the Blue Wool Scale. The latter operates from one to eight, one being extremely poor light fastness and eight being the maximum light fastness possible.

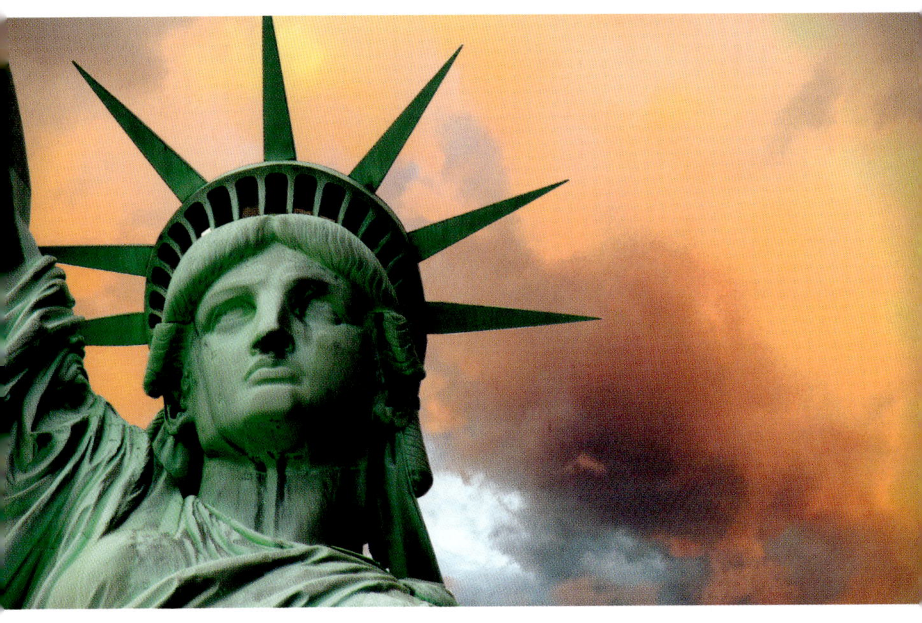

The Statue of Liberty (1886) is made of copper and was originally brown. However, exposure of the copper to the elements and the polluted air resulted in a reaction that oxidized the copper and produced the iconic green color by the early twentieth century.

76 POINTILLISM

A painting technique in which small, distinct dots of color are applied to form an image

- Pointillism emerged toward the end of the nineteenth century and is primarily associated with the artists Georges Seurat and Paul Signac. While Impressionism was an attempt by artists to represent their subjective responses, Pointillism was a post-Impressionist movement that involved a more technical approach.

- When different colors of paint are mixed, an inherent loss in chroma results in some dullness. Pointillists avoided this dulling by placing dots of unmixed paint on the canvas close to one another so that the dots would be blended by the eye to create more striking colors.

- Pointillism is sometimes referred to as Divisionism, but there is a distinction. Pointillist paintings are done primarily with dots of paint; Divisionist paintings are done using short strokes.

- The method by which modern devices mix red, green, and blue light to create emissive displays is based on a similar principle, albeit on a smaller scale, so that the individual dots cannot be seen by the naked eye.

SEE ALSO Impressionism • Partitive Mixture

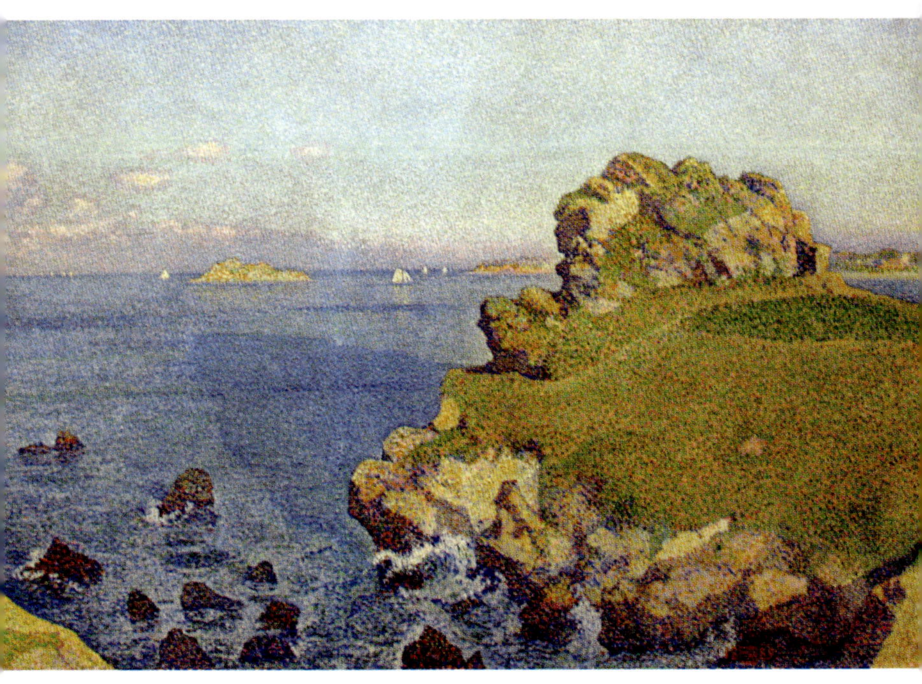

The 'Per-Kiridy' at High Tide (1889), by Théo van Rysselberghe.

77 PRIMARY COLORS

A set of colored lights or colorants that can be combined to generate a range of different colors

- It is often said that three color primaries can be mixed together to create any color, but this is not true. It is possible to create any hue, but there is inevitable loss of chroma or saturation when mixing colorants or colored lights, respectively.

- The largest range (or gamut) of colors that can be created with three light primaries occurs with red, green, and blue lights. For that reason, most emissive devices, such as computer and phone displays, use these primaries. However, there is some variability among devices and manufacturers in the actual choice of red, green, and blue. This is one reason for lack of color fidelity in imaging systems.

- Optimal subtractive primaries are red-absorbing (cyan), green-absorbing (magenta), and blue-absorbing (yellow) colorants. In printing, a four-primary system consisting of cyan, magenta, yellow, and black is ubiquitous. At least three primaries are required in order to generate all hues.

The identification of primary colors in any system is determined by economics based on choosing the fewest colors that result in the largest gamut.

SEE ALSO Additive Mixture • CMYK • Gamuts • Munsell System • RGB • Subtractive Mixture

DEVICE-DEPENDENT PRIMARY COLORS

It is often claimed that the digital primaries of the monitor (RGB) are the complements of the process primaries of the printer (CMY) and vice versa. Although this is a popular concept, it is not accurate. Examples of process cyan and process magenta should be taken as representative of the physical colorants employed for printing, as distinct from the secondary colors of the RGB monitor colors, often called cyan and magenta, which are distinctly greener and more purple, respectively.

Note that because hue angle (H) is defined using nonlinear RGB, opposite hue angles are not exact additive complementaries except on the R-Cyan, G-Magenta, and B-Yellow axes.

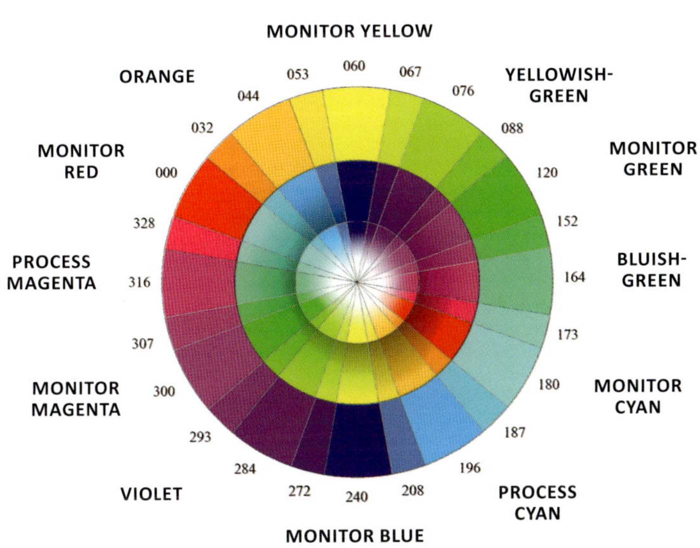

78 RAYLEIGH SCATTERING

The scattering of light by the molecules and particles in air

- Matter interacts with light in several ways. Light may be absorbed, transmitted, or scattered. When light is scattered, it changes direction. When light interacts with particles that are small (up to about a tenth of the wavelength of light), the scattering that occurs is referred to as Rayleigh scattering. This is distinct from Mie scattering that occurs with larger particles, such as pigment particles in paint.

- Rayleigh scattering, named after the nineteenth-century physicist Lord Rayleigh (1842–1919), most commonly occurs in gases. The sky is blue because of Rayleigh scattering of light by the atmosphere. Rayleigh scattering affects short-wavelength light much more than long-wavelength; therefore, it is blue light from the sun that is scattered by the atmosphere and travels toward our eyes.

- Rayleigh scattering also explains the red and yellow in the sky at sunrise or sunset. In this case, the light traveling from the sun is the short-wavelength light that is removed from the light that reaches us.

SEE ALSO Atmospheric Perspective • Electromagnetic Spectrum • Nature's Light

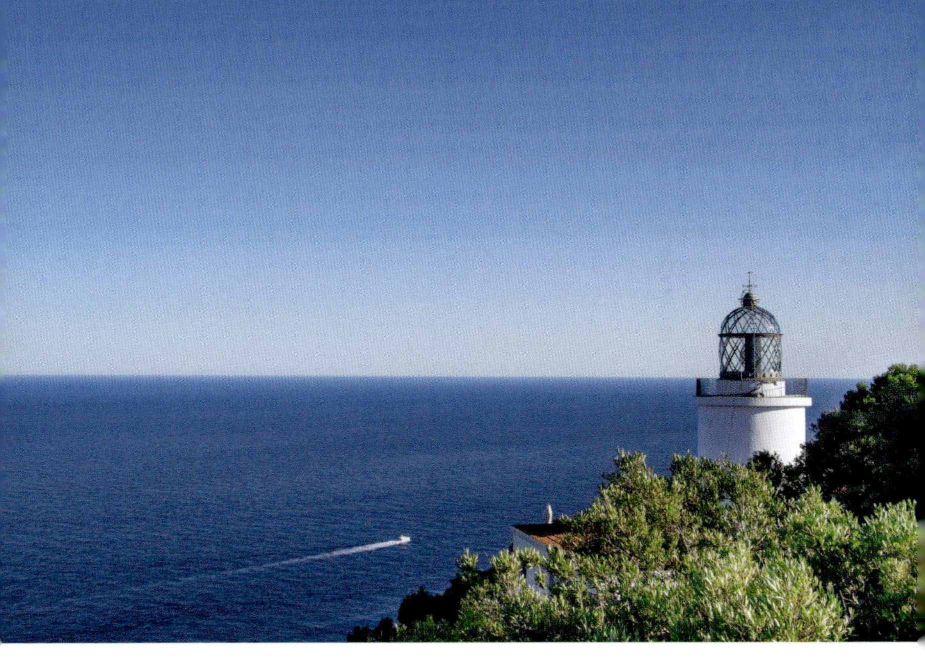

Rayleigh scattering is responsible for the blue color of the sky. The shorter wavelengths of light from the sun are deflected by particles in the atmosphere and reach our eyes. The color of the ocean is blue because it reflects the color of the sky and because longer wavelengths of light are absorbed more strongly than shorter wavelengths by water.

79 RGB

The red, green, and blue lights used in additive mixture

- In the digital world RGB (red/green/blue) specification of color is ubiquitous, but there is no single RGB standard. In most systems, a color is represented by 256 levels of each RGB, which leads to about sixteen million combinations. Each RGB value is an integer in the range 0–255. This level of precision is more than sufficient for most consumer applications, although some specialist displays and cameras allow a greater degree of what is referred to as bit depth.

- There is wide variability in the primaries used by different devices. This means that if we display the same RGB values on two different displays, we will probably see two different colors. Color management is the process of working to compensate for this device dependency to achieve color fidelity.

- Of the standard RGB color spaces that exist, RGB is particularly important in modern digital imaging systems. Its widespread adoption by manufacturers enables a good degree of color fidelity despite the variability among devices.

SEE ALSO Additive Mixture • Color Management

Hex color is code for RGB. In this system the 0–255 decimal values of each RGB value are represented by two characters in the hexadecimal system. In the example at right, the hexadecimal red value of 97 corresponds to 151 in decimal (9*16 + 7). The advantage of this system is that every color is represented by only six characters.

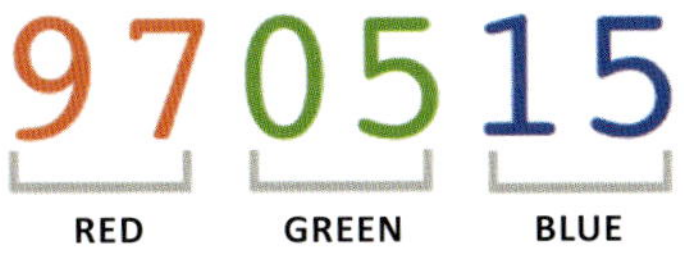

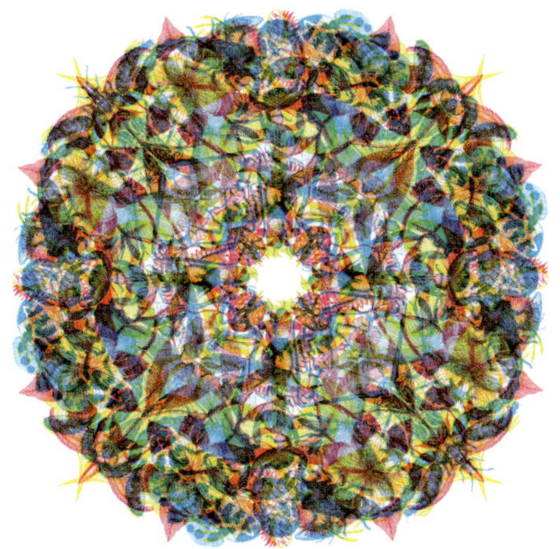

Rosone N.3 (2010), by Francesco Rugi and Silvia Quintanilla, known collectively as Carnovsky. Designs for wallpaper and other products are printed in layers of CMY, which separate when viewed under RGB lights or filters.

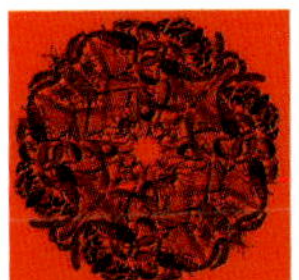

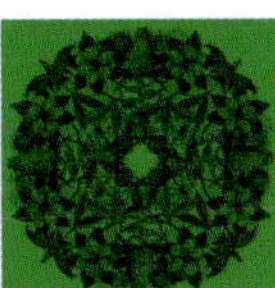

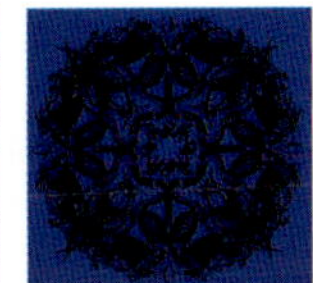

80 SAFETY COLORS

Standardized colors used to communicate levels of safety

- The consistent use of color can enable us to identify hazards quickly and reliably. The American National Standards Institute (ANSI) 2535 has established specific color-safety meanings:

    - **RED** = fire protection, danger of injury or death, and emergency stop
    - **ORANGE** = moderate risk of injury
    - **YELLOW** = minor risk of injury and caution statements
    - **GREEN** = safety equipment and first-aid equipment

- Fluorescent yellow and orange are used extensively for clothing because of their high visibility. Fluorescent dyes enable a material to absorb light at certain wavelengths and then re-emit the light at a longer wavelength. This can increase the intensity of the light emitted in the orange or yellow region of the spectrum.

An important worldwide use of colors in safety is the classic red for stop and green for go in traffic lights and railway signals, as well as in shipping and aeronautics.

SEE ALSO Color Meaning • Fluorescence

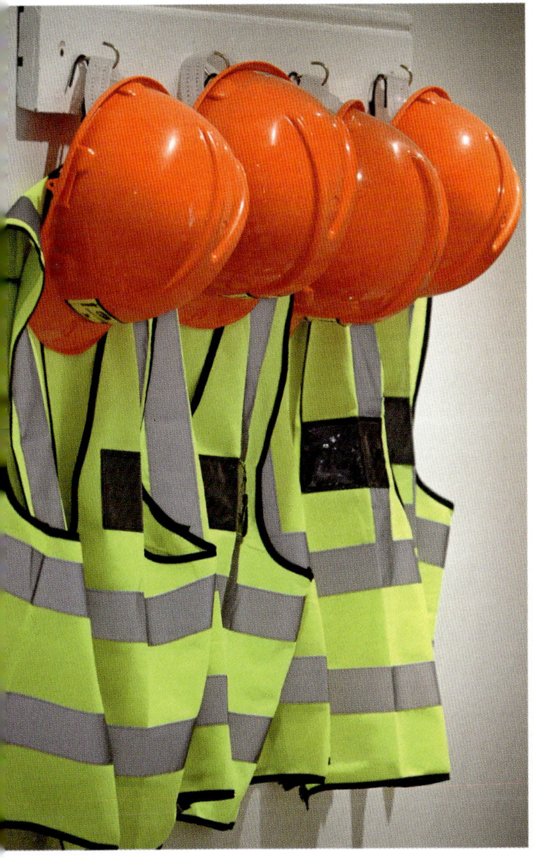

ANSI Safety Red PMS 186C Munsell 7.5R 4/14	#bd2024
ANSI Safety Orange PMS 151C Munsell 5YR 6/15	#ff7900
ANSI Safety Yellow PMS 109C Munsell 5Y 8/12	#ffe100
ANSI Safety Blue PMS 285C Munsell 2.5PB 3.5/10	#004488

ANSI Z535.1-2017: Safety Colors.
RGB within Allowable Tolerance.

Examples of safety colors as defined by the American National Standards Institute (ANSI).

Fluorescent yellow is one of the ANSI/ISEA colors approved for safety vests.

81 SHADOWS

Areas where the light from a light source is completely or partially obstructed by an object

- In addition to giving objects their form, the type of lighting and shape of the object determine the nature of a shadow and affect color perception. The range between the darkest and lightest areas affects the overall effect of an image.

- Cast shadow: created by an object blocking the light source. It has a hard edge close to the object that becomes softer the farther it is from the object.

- Core shadow: on the surface of an object opposite the light source; lighter than a cast shadow, with a softer edge. Depending surface's shape, it can be a gradient.

- Crevice shadow: the darkest one in the space opposite the light source, between the object and the surface.

- Highlight: the lightest spot on the surface where the light is focused.

- Penumbra: area of partial shadow between the cast shadow and full illumination.

In computer graphics, shadow rendering or mapping is the process of adding shadows by using the light's point of view.

SEE ALSO Chiaroscuro • Gradients

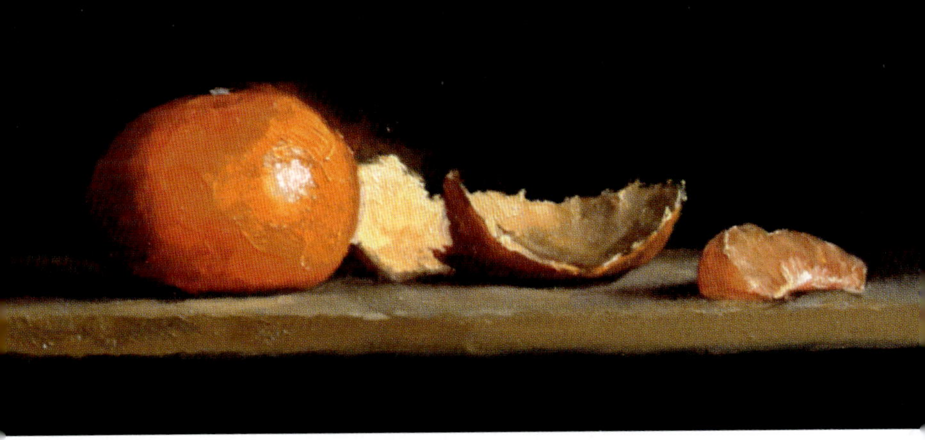

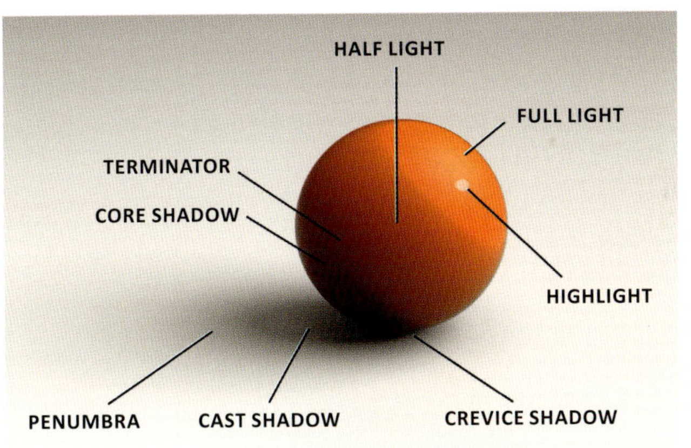

Painting by Paul Foxton.

Shadow terms.

82 SIMULTANEOUS CONTRAST

A perceptual shift in color that occurs when a color appears to move toward the opposite color of the surround against which it is seen

- Color is a perception and relative in nature. The appearance of a color can change depending on the conditions in which it is viewed. In simultaneous contrast, two colors placed side by side contrast with each other by appearing to take on the attributes of the opposing hue.

- If a nominally gray patch is placed on a red background, it will contrast with the red and appear greenish or cyanish. On a blue background, it will appear yellowish. (There can also be contrast in lightness and/or chroma.)

- Contrast occurs because of the way in which the human visual system processes light information. Cone responses from one part of a scene are effectively compared with cone responses from neighboring parts of the scene, resulting spatially relative in color perception.

In addition to retinal processing, higher-level cognitive processes may play a role in contrast effects; research is ongoing.

SEE ALSO Albers's *Interaction of Color* • Bezold Effect • Human Visual System • Successive Contrast

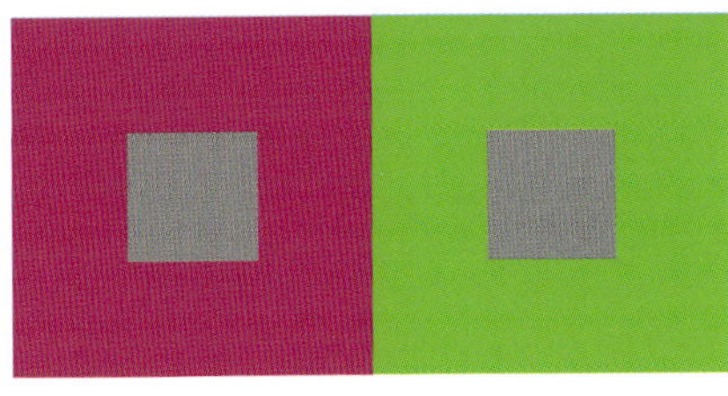

Hue contrast: In the Albers style image, the two small squares are physically the same but look different because of the different hue backgrounds.

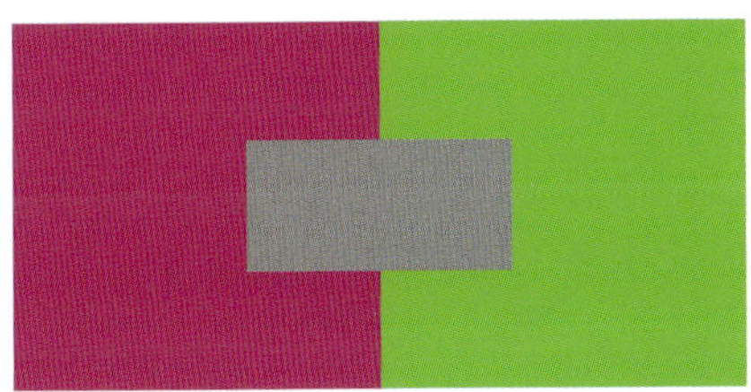

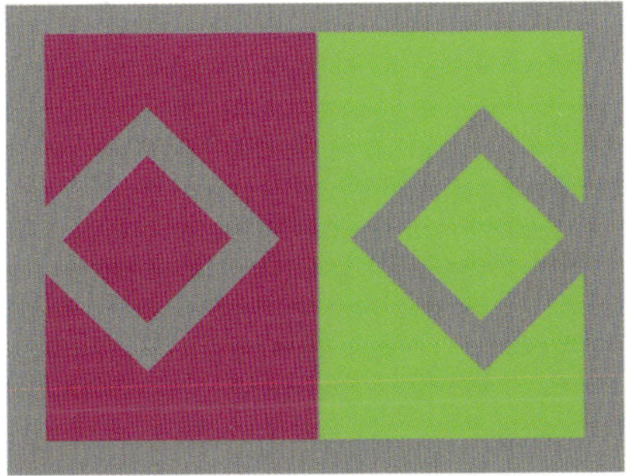

Hue contrast: The same colors are used in this image, designed by Paul Green-Armytage to heighten the contrast effect.

83 SPECTRAL HUES

Hues that are present in the spectrum of colors produced by splitting sunlight with, for example, a prism

- The range of wavelengths visible to humans is approximately 360 nm to 780 nm. Seen together, these wavelengths appear white. If we consider single or narrow bands of wavelengths from this range, we typically perceive bands of color. These are known as the spectral hues and include reds, oranges, yellows, greens, cyans, blues, and violets. We experience this phenomenon whenever we see a rainbow in the sky or when light is passed through a glass prism.

- The spectral hues such as yellow can be produced from single wavelengths or from an additive mixture of other wavelengths. For example, a mixture of red and green lights can make yellow.

- Other hues, such as purples, magentas, and violet reds, do not occur in the spectrum. These nonspectral hues occur only when we see several short and long wavelengths of light coincidently. For example, if we additively mix short (bluish) and long (reddish) light, we can see purples and magentas.

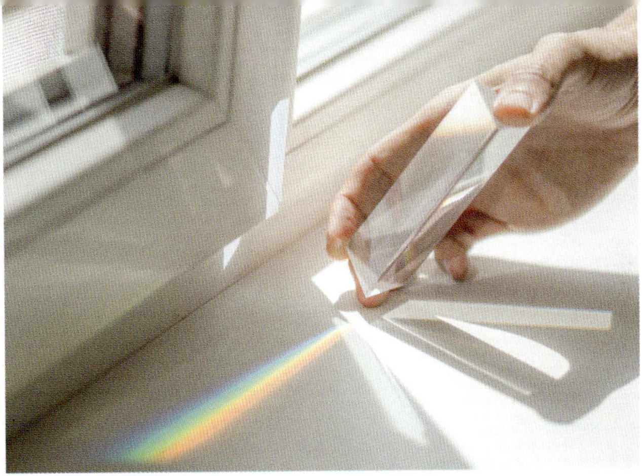

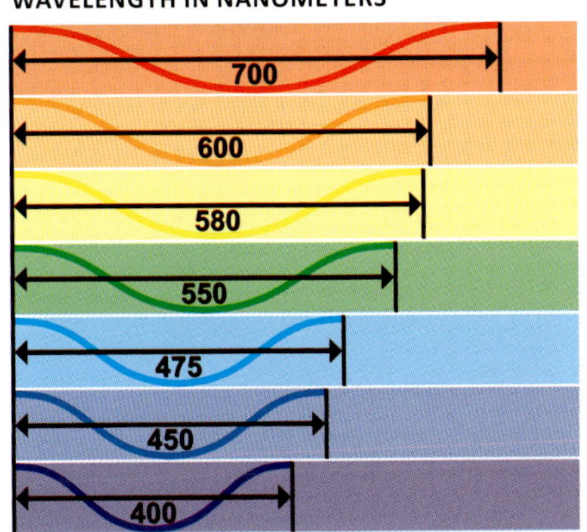

A prism splits sunlight into wavelengths measured in nanometers from 400 nm to 700 nm. In the graphic below, 400 nm (purple) represent gamma rays; 450 nm (indigo) x-rays; 475 nm (blue).

WAVELENGTH IN NANOMETERS

 STRUCTURAL COLOR

Animals produce color from three main sources: pigments, bioluminescence, and structure

- Structural characteristics can lead to scattering of light. One example is human eye color. Brown occurs in those who have high concentrations of the pigment melanin, which primarily absorbs the long visible wavelengths. In the absence of melanin, the structural components of the eye scatter light and cause blue eyes.

- Butterfly wings and peacock feathers are examples of structural color in nature. When structures result in light scattering, it can produce a blue color or, in conjunction with pigments, a wide range of colors.

- Structural color has been studied since the introduction of the electron microscope in the 1940s. In addition to scattering and diffraction, highly magnified images of natural structures led to an understanding of interference, in which thin layers of a material, with the distance between them typically like the wavelength of light, can produce unusual color effects like those in soap bubbles.

Our understanding of structural color phenomena has led to commercial applications, including antireflection coatings on lenses in eyeglasses, binoculars, and telescopes.

SEE ALSO Electromagnetic Spectrum • Rayleigh Scattering

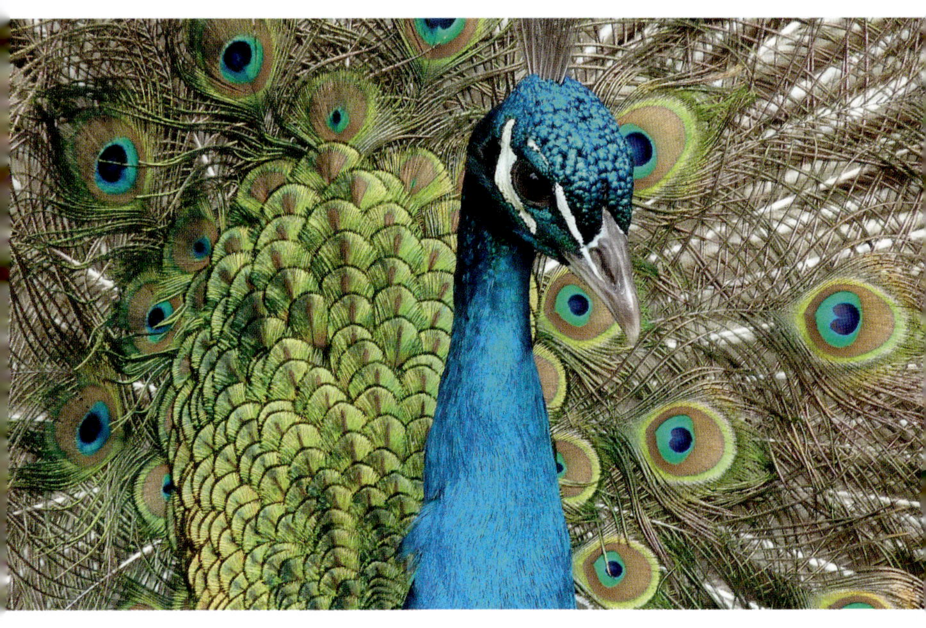

In peacock feathers the main colorant is a brown pigment. This is supplemented by structural aspects, which can result in a wide variety of vivid colors.

85 SUBTRACTIVE MIXTURE

The process and effect of combining colorants such as paints, inks, and dyes

- The term *subtractive* arises because colorants absorb (subtract) light. The light that is not absorbed is the light that we see.

- Traditional color theory teaches that the subtractive primaries are red, yellow, and blue. In modern process printing, the primaries are cyan, magenta, and yellow. Both result in subtractive mixtures. Contrary to both color theories, paints or inks of these sets of colors cannot be combined to create all other colors.

- A loss of chroma occurs when two colorants of different hues are mixed. Starting with six primaries rather than three can offset the loss in a subtractive mixture. Variations of this concept include using two each of red, yellow, and blue (known as double or split primary systems). Another method is adding orange, green, and violet (often called a secondary palette in paint) or an extended gamut (in printing).

Additive and subtractive color mixing are related. The optimal additive primaries are red, green, and blue, and the optimal subtractive primaries are red-absorbing (cyan), green-absorbing (magenta), and blue-absorbing (yellow) colorants.

SEE ALSO Additive Mixture • CMYK • Color Management • RGB

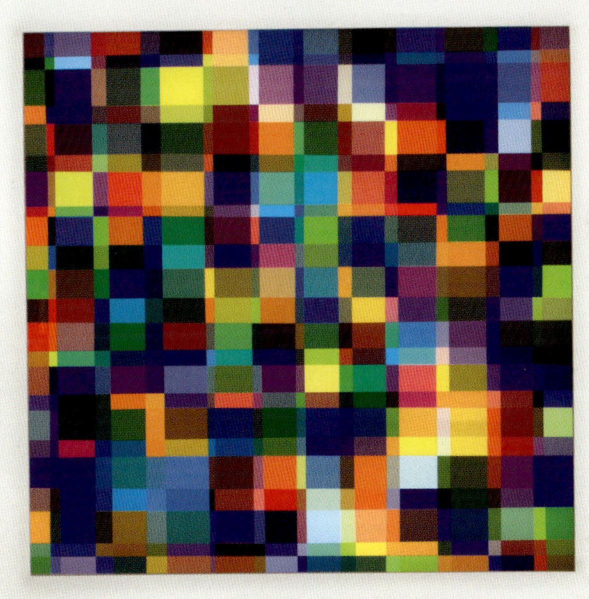

Color Test (576) (2017), by Spencer Finch. LED lightbox, Fujitrans.

The Color Tests are made by layering and laminating two translucent grids of unique colors printed on Fujitrans to form a more complex grid with more complex colors. The overlapping gels result in subtractive mixtures.

86 SUCCESSIVE CONTRAST

A temporal effect in which retinal impressions persist following the removal of a stimulus, and color perception is influenced by the colors that were previously seen

- If a red swatch is stared at for a short while and then removed to reveal a neutral or white background, the viewer will observe a weak green or cyan color in its place. This effect, one perception of color followed by another, is commonly known as the afterimage.

- Afterimage colors are the opposites of the optical colors that are originally viewed. They occur when the eyes' cones adapt to overstimulation and lose sensitivity. For example, looking at a red swatch stimulates the long-wavelength-sensitive cones; when the swatch is removed, these cones will be less sensitive and a white background will appear to have a cyan or greenish color.

It is important to consider your state of visual adaptation when making any critical color evaluations. Let your eyes rest for a few minutes following color observations.

SEE ALSO Human Visual System • Simultaneous Contrast

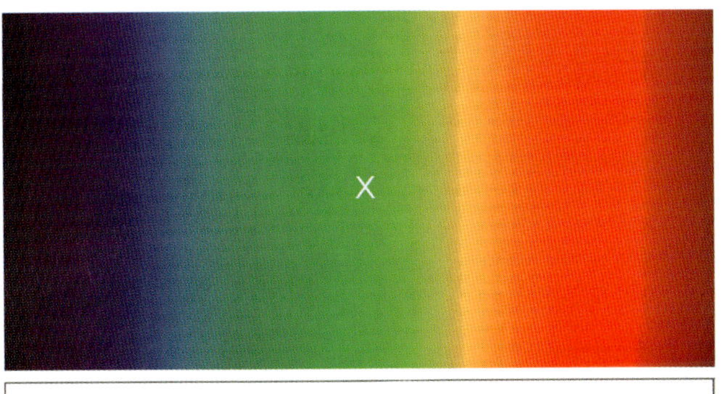

Stare at the X on the top for thirty to forty-five seconds. Try to relax and not move your eyes. Then look at the X in the white space below the image. It may take as long as ten seconds, and blinking may help. Try it again but keep one eye covered or closed. When the afterimage colors appear, open your covered eye at the same time you cover your other eye. Go back and forth covering each eye. What happens to the afterimage?

87 SUSTAINABLE COLOR

Efforts to reduce the environmental impact of petroleum-based dyes by developing economical natural colorants

- There is a growing awareness of the environmental impact of manufacturing products using synthetic textiles, dyes, and food colorants. Efforts are underway to produce affordable sustainable colorants from natural sources.

- The first synthetic color was mauveine, a derivative of coal tar discovered by William Henry Perkin in 1856. Today 99% of the colorants used in industrial applications come from fossil fuels. The textile industry is responsible for 20% of global water pollution, due to the toxicity of synthetic dyes and their resistance to biodegradation.

- There are three types of natural dyes: plant based (such as woad and indigo), animal based (such as cochineal and murex sea snails), and mineral based (such as ochre and lapis lazuli). Biotech researchers are experimenting with manufacturing natural colorants from fungi, algae, and bacteria for use not only in textiles but also in foods, drugs, and cosmetics.

An aesthetic decision to use natural materials can also be a sustainable choice.

SEE ALSO Color Literacy • Environmental Color Design • Geography of Color

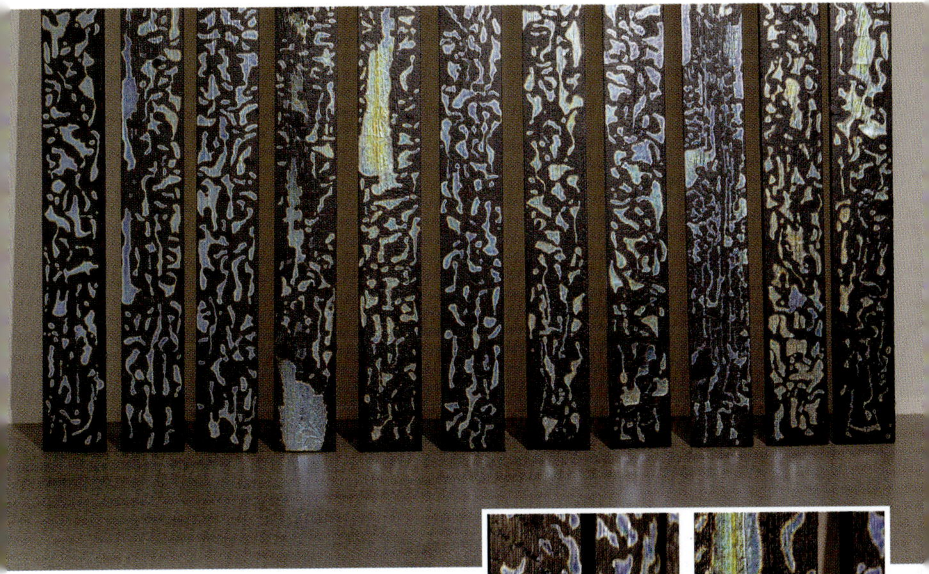

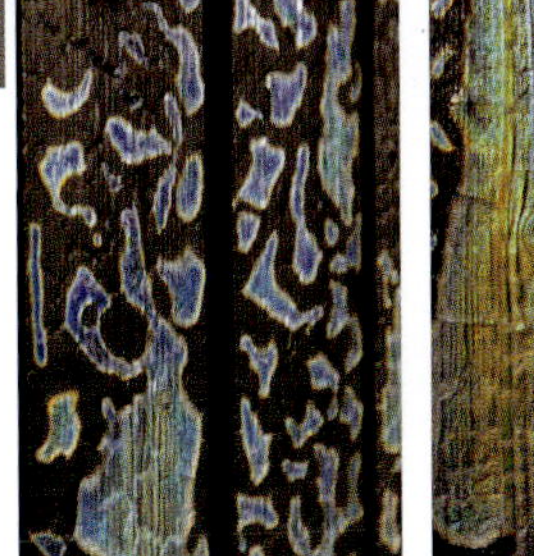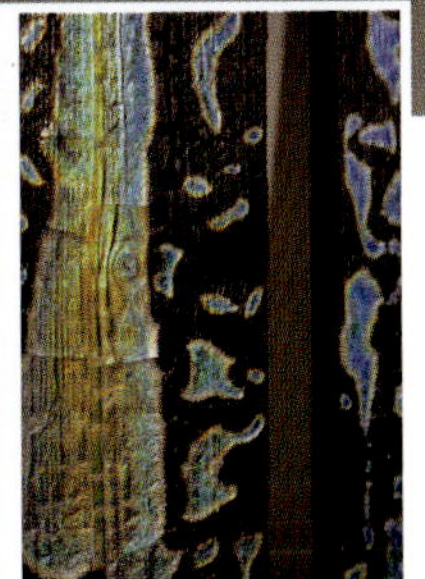

Shimmering Wood (2022), by Konrad Klockars and Noora Yau. Sustainable structural color produced 100 percent from wood and applied on wood as a result of research at Aalto University's Structural Color Studio in Finland.

88 SYMBOLIC COLOR

Color intentionally used to communicate meaning based on individual, cultural, or universal associations

- Color symbolism is context-dependent, influenced by changes over time across cultures around the world. Although there are few universal standards for colors as symbols with specific meanings—stop-sign red is an exception—there are common themes.

- Symbolic representations of religious concepts or articles may include a specific color with which the concept or object is associated. There is evidence to suggest that colors have been used for ceremonial purposes as early as 90,000 BC.

- Diversity in color symbolism occurs because color meanings and symbolism evolve over time on an individual and cultural basis. Contemporary examples of evolving symbolism include the colors adopted by sports teams, organized movements, and social causes such as breast cancer awareness.

SEE ALSO Brand Colors • Color Meaning • Emotion and Color

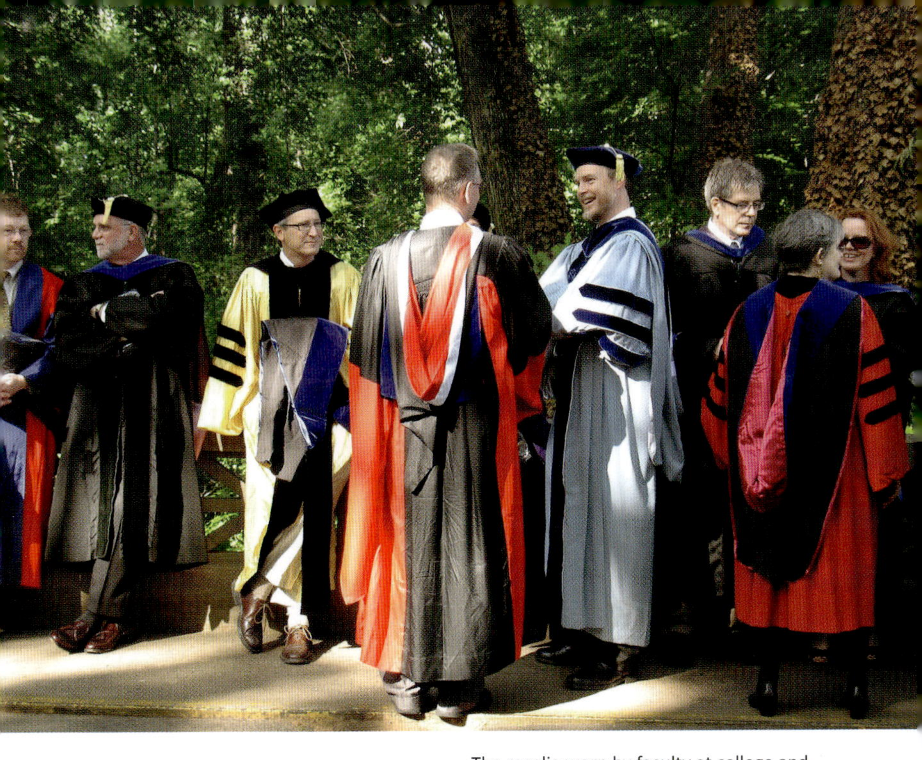

The regalia worn by faculty at college and university graduation ceremonies is an example of symbolic color.

89 SYNESTHESIA

The phenomenon whereby stimulation of one sensory pathway, such as hearing, leads to involuntary experiences in another sensory pathway, such as vision

- Interest in synesthesia goes back to Ancient Greece, and interest in the association between music and color remains to this day. Although research is expanding, the neurological cause of the condition is still unclear.

- The most common type is grapheme-color synesthesia, in which people perceive letters/numbers as being inherently colored. Chromesthesia is a color-related condition in which everyday sounds or certain musical notes can trigger the perception of color.

- Synesthesia may be a source of creativity in artists, one example being painter Wassily Kandinsky, who famously associated colors with shapes.

- While some art is created by synesthetes, some is intended to evoke synesthetic associations in non-synesthetic viewers. The most famous example is the 1940 animated Disney film *Fantasia*.

Although synesthetes tend to have different associations from one another, there are some general consistencies and participants are usually consistent with their own associations.

SEE ALSO Emotion and Color • Human Visual System

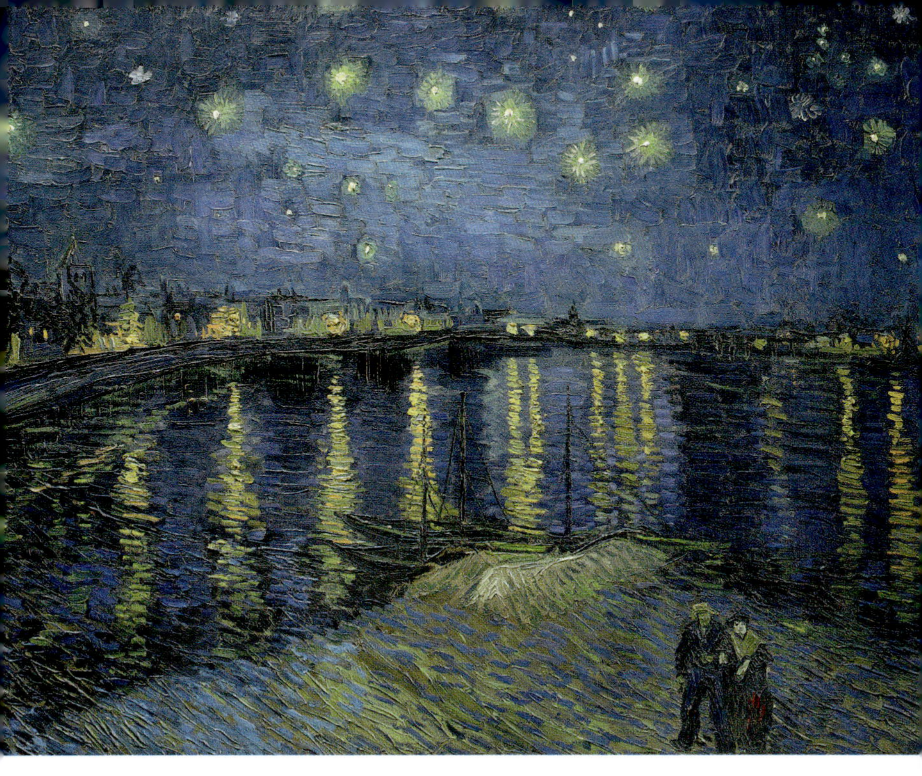

Starry Night Over the Rhone (1888), by Vincent van Gogh.

Many art historians believe that Vincent van Gogh had a form of synesthesia called chromesthesia—an experience of the senses where the person associates sounds with colors.

90 TECHNICOLOR

An important development in the 1930s that led to a rapid increase in the use of color in the movie industry

- The first color movies were produced in the first quarter of the twentieth century with the Kinemacolor process, inspired by discoveries made by James Clerk Maxwell. The original Kinemacolor process was an additive system that used only two color primaries, red and green.

- Between 1920 and 1930, Technicolor dominated the film industry. There were several systems. Technicolor I was similar to Kinemacolor and used a two-primary additive system. Technicolor II, III, and IV incorporated developments that would lead to a trichromatic subtractive system that could produce beautiful and vivid color images.

- In the 1930s, Walt Disney used Technicolor in movies such as *Flowers and Trees and Three Little Pigs*. The full, live-action gamut of Technicolor was unleashed in 1939 with MGM's *The Wizard of Oz*.

Today the use of color in the movie industry has shifted to digital technologies, but some directors still prefer shooting on film.

SEE ALSO Cinematic Color • Gamuts • Palettes

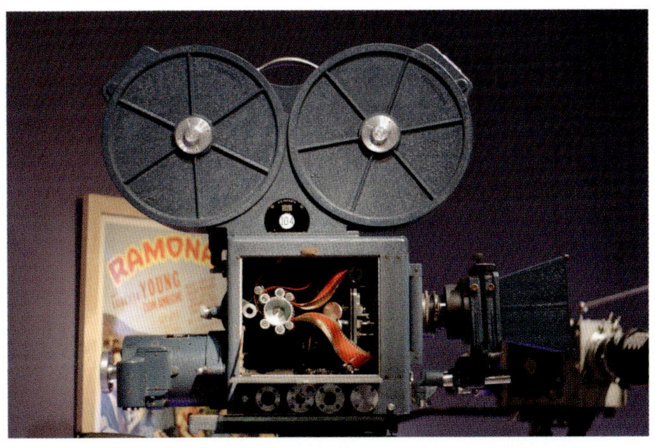

A 3-strip Technicolor camera from the 1930s. Two strips of 35 mm black and white film negative, one sensitive to blue light and the other to red light, ran together through an aperture behind a magenta filter, which allowed blue and red light to pass through. A third film strip of black and white film negative ran through a separate aperture, behind a green filter.

The Wizard of Oz showcased the capabilities of Technicolor.

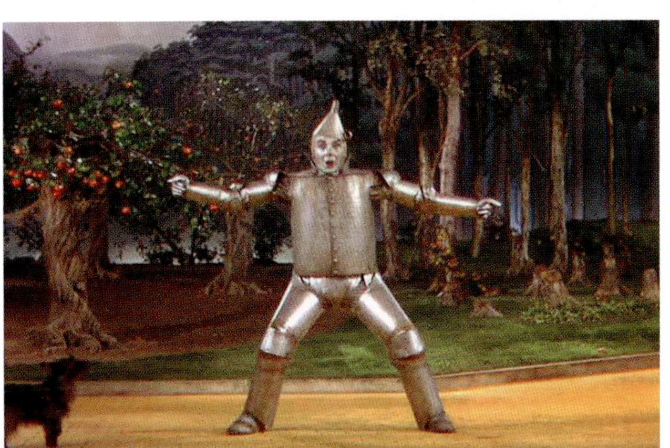

189

Surface characteristics of objects affect the perception of color

- Texture is a key element of art and design. Everything has texture, both physical and visual. The term is often described in words such as *rough* or *smooth*, *hard* or *soft*, *matte* or *glossy*.

- Physical texture is the tactile quality of an object. It can be touched and felt. The texture of surfaces interacts with light and affects the perception of the color.

ATTRIBUTES OF APPEARANCE

- *Cesia* is a term for the aspect of visual appearance related to the perception of different spatial distributions of light. The word was proposed by Cesar Jannello in the 1980s. It is the same type of phenomenon that Robert Hunt called *geometric attributes of appearance*. These surface attributes affect the perception of color.

- Light that is not absorbed by an object may be reflected either sharply (mirrored) or diffusely (matte). Materials also interact differently with light depending on whether they are more or less transparent, translucent, or opalescent and, of course, in different levels of darkness according to the light-dark axis.

SEE ALSO Context • Local Color

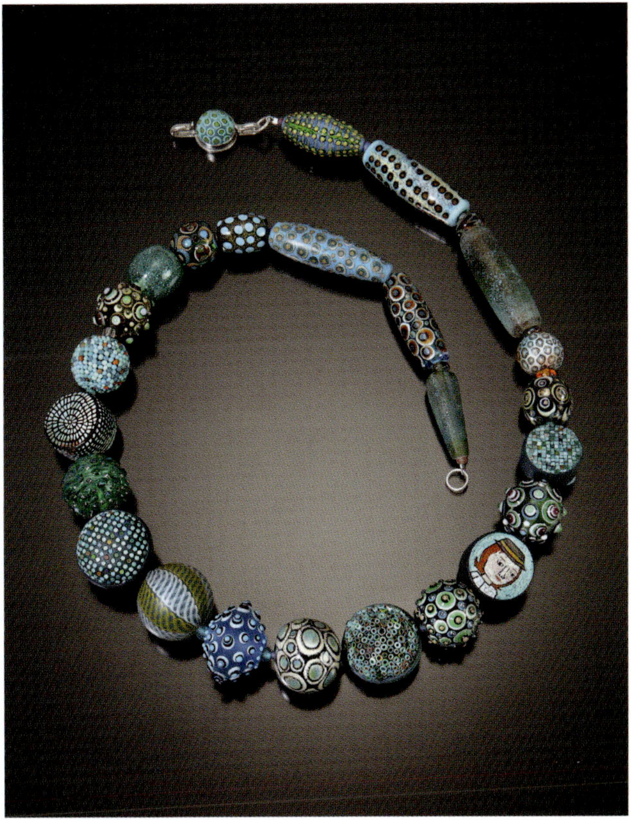

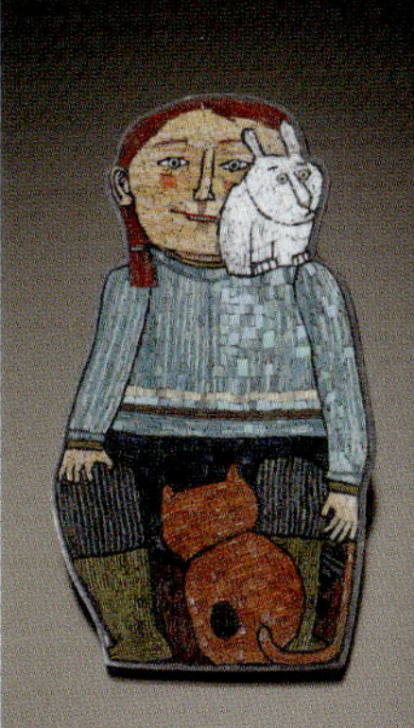

Texture is a key element in the work | of contemporary art jewelers Cynthia Toops and Dan Adams.

(Left) Necklace (2020). Polymer, glass, by Cynthia Toops and Dan Adams.

(Above) Micromosaic Brooch (1.5" x 3.5" tall). Polymer, silver, by Cynthia Toops.

THREE DIMENSIONS OF COLOR

Colors can be described according to attributes scaled in three dimensions: hue, lightness, and chroma—or similar terms

- Although the terminology varies depending on the discipline, the three attributes of color are:

    1. **HUE**

    2. **LIGHTNESS** (value, brightness)

    3. **CHROMA** (colorfulness, chromaticness, saturation, intensity)

- Hue is the degree to which a color looks red, yellow, green, or blue. Lightness is the variation in the color from dark to light. Chroma describes the visual power of a color from strong to weak.

- Black, white, and a full range of light to dark grays are achromatic colors—that is, colors that contain no chroma.

- The 3D nature of color is often represented as a color space, as it is in the Munsell, RAL, and Natural Color Systems.

Even though there are other appearance attributes that affect how we perceive the world—for example, objects can be opaque, translucent, or glossy—the topic of color in three dimensions is normally restricted to the attributes of hue, lightness, and chroma.

SEE ALSO Human Visual System • Munsell System • Natural Color System

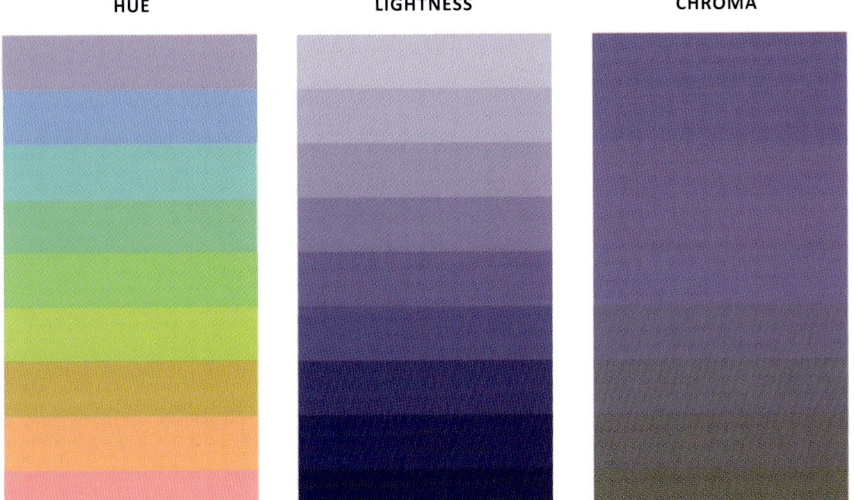

Examples of the range of each of the three attributes of color that are organized in 3D models.

93 TINT, SHADE, AND TONE

Variations of pure hues made by mixing with white, black, and gray

- Traditionally, color theory has used the terms *tint*, *shade*, and *tone* to define a method of mixing hues with white, gray, or black pigments to create a larger gamut of monochromatic colors. Therefore, these terms have very specific meanings for artists.

- In this methodology, tint refers to the colors that result from mixing a hue pigment with a white pigment; tone refers to the colors that result from mixing a hue pigment with a light, medium, or dark gray pigment; shade refers to the colors that result from mixing with a black pigment.

  - Tinting a vivid color results in colors that are described as pale.
  - Toning a vivid color results in colors that are described as muted.
  - Shading a vivid color results in colors that are described as dark.

Any color, not just vivid colors, can be tinted, shaded, and toned.

SEE ALSO Character Zones • Color Meaning • Subtractive Mixture
• Three Dimensions of Color

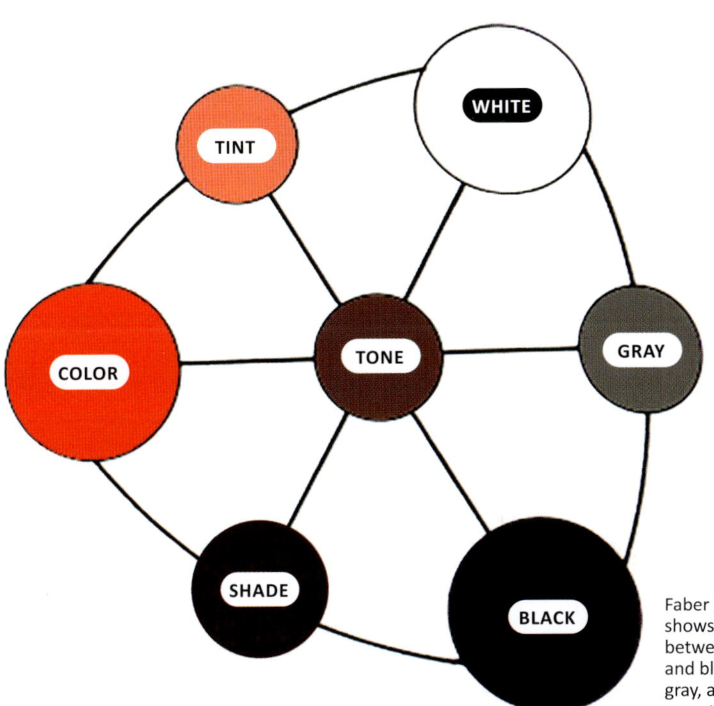

Faber Birren's triangle shows the relationship between the pure hues and black, white, and gray, as well as three ways to mix a tone.

TINT = Color + White

SHADE = Color + Black

TONE = Color + Gray, Tint + Black, Shade + White

94 TRADITIONAL COLOR THEORY

An ambiguously defined body of knowledge that has been traditionally taught in art and design schools for many decades

- Although the exact curriculum is not precisely defined, traditional color theory typically includes some or all the following topics: color naming, color mixing, color circles, color harmony, and color meaning.

- A great many people contributed to the ideas that are traditionally taught as color theory. For example, Goethe, Michel Eugène Chevreul, Wilhelm Ostwald, Albert H. Munsell, and Johannes Itten all made important contributions to a topic referred to as color harmony, which concerns the aesthetic relationships between colors. Itten was particularly influential on the concept of hue circle and the use of this tool to teach aspects of color harmony and color mixing.

- The STEAM (Science, Technology, Engineering, the Arts and Mathematics) movement is an opportunity to align color teaching in the arts with state-of-the-art science and technologies.

Many concepts in traditional color theory can be expanded to reflect the topics and technologies relevant in the twenty-first century.

SEE ALSO Additive Mixture • Color Harmony • Subtractive Mixture

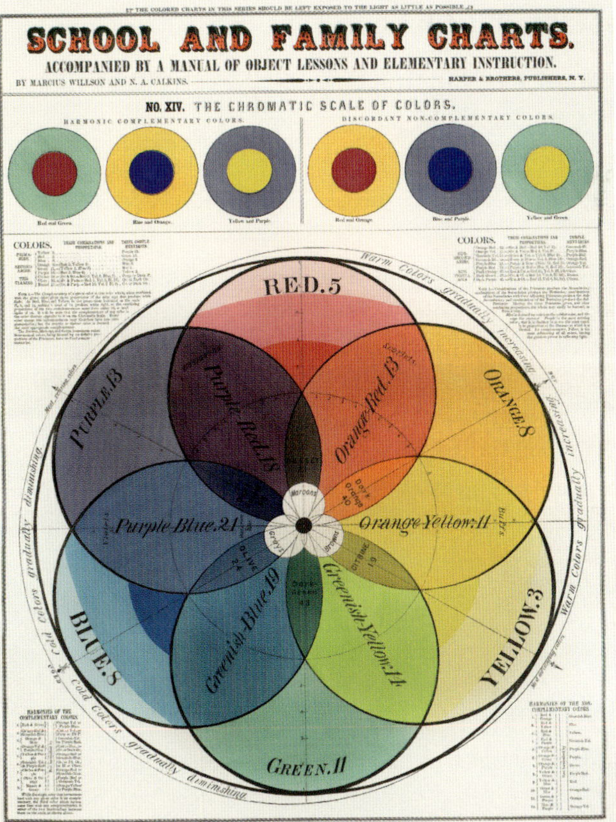

The elements of traditional color theory as shown on a classroom poster from 1890.

TRANSPARENCY EFFECT

The pictorial illusion of overlapping transparent layers to represent multiple perspectives

- In literal transparency, a transparent material allows light to pass through, so the viewer sees what is behind it. The illusion of transparency is the use of colors and shapes to suggest overlapping planes and multiple viewpoints.

- Renaissance and Baroque painters used transparent layers of paint to create nuanced surface effects for skin tones, atmospheric conditions, and fabrics. In the early twentieth century, the Cubists used the illusion of transparency to build up visual layers representing objects shifting in space and time. Modernist painters used transparency to add the illusion of depth to compositions made with flat planes of color.

- There are three types of transparency effects:

    - Two colors can both appear transparent with the illusion of material behind them.
    - One color can appear to be transparent on top of the second, which appears opaque.
    - The relationship of colors can be ambiguous with no visual clue about which color is on top of the other.

The element of ambiguity is critical to the success of transparency effects aiming to represent multiple perspectives.

SEE ALSO Advancing and Receding

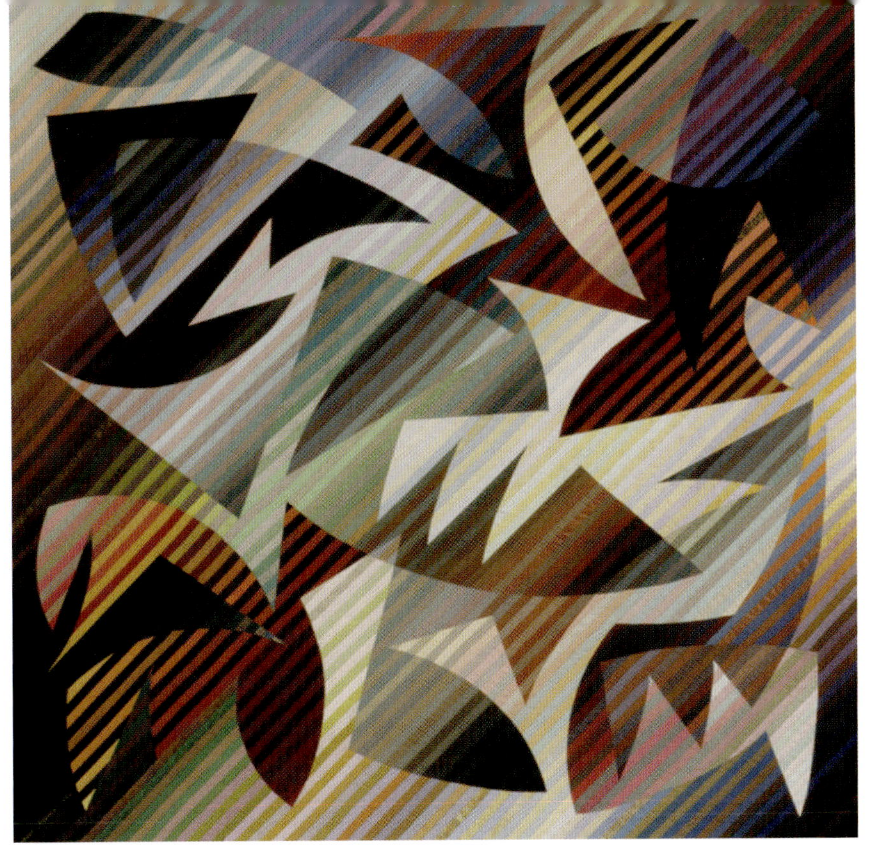

The Metaphysics of Action (Entropic Forms) (1994), a contemporary art quilt by Michael James.

 TRICHROMACY

Human vision is mediated by three types of light-reception cells, called cones, in the retina of the eye

- Most of us have three types of cone cells in the eye, which is why it is possible to generate a wide range of colors (and all hues) using three lights or three colorants in mixture. Some people have only two classes of cone cells, and this is one of the most frequent causes of so-called color blindness, where people can see color but have limited color discrimination ability.

- Toward the end of the twentieth century, it was discovered that some people—almost always female—have four types of cone cells. There is some evidence that these tetrachromats may have enhanced color discrimination. Tetrachromacy is also commonly found in many species of fish and birds.

- Tetrachromacy may not always be an advantage. Color imaging technologies, such as cinematography and emissive displays, are predicated on the idea of trichromacy and may not work so well for tetrachromats.

SEE ALSO Human Visual System • Limited Color Vision • Synesthesia

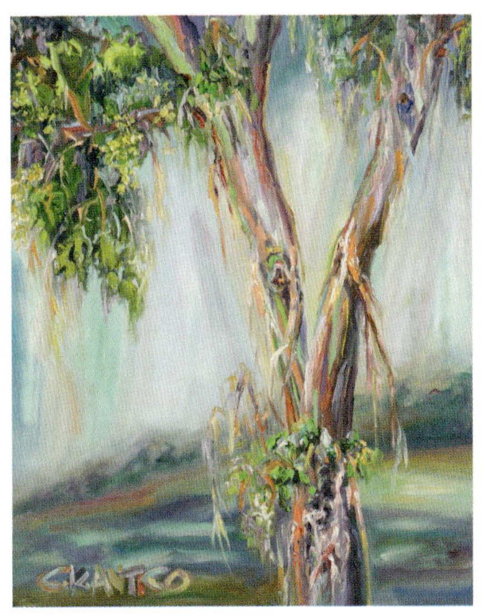 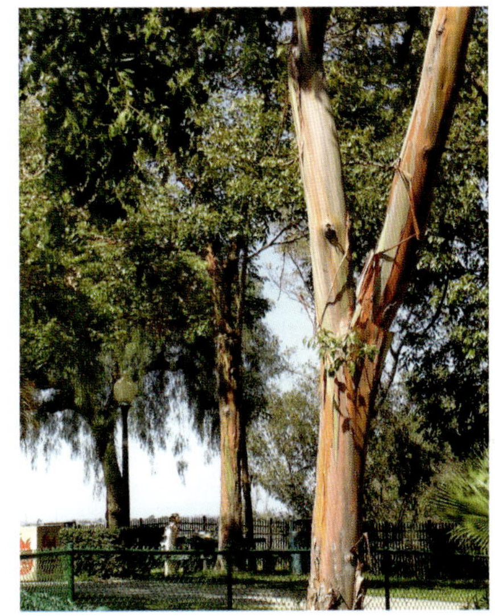

TETROCHROMACY

Rainbow Eucalyptus (2016).

Oil painting by the artist and tetrachromat Concetta Antico with a photo of the same species of tree by Robert Linsdell.

97 UNDERTONE

The underlying hue of a low-chroma colored sample

- Colors can be described using terms such as *lightness*, *chroma*, and *hue*. The hue of most samples can be described by name—for example, red, yellow, or green. However, for samples of low chroma it can be difficult to identify the underlying hue.

- In several industries, notably cosmetics and interior design, the term *undertone* is often used to describe the hue of a sample. In cosmetics, many people have an undertone between red and yellow. People with a redder undertone have a hue angle less than about forty-five degrees, and those with a yellow-greener undertone have a hue angle greater than forty-five degrees.

- In the paint industry, near-neutral paints are popular for use in offices and homes. There, the term *undertone* is often used to differentiate between different near-neutral samples.

The undertone is sometimes described as warm or cool, but this can be misleading because the appearance of color is relative to the context such as the lighting and surrounding colors.

SEE ALSO Hue Angle • Near Neutrals • Warm and Cool

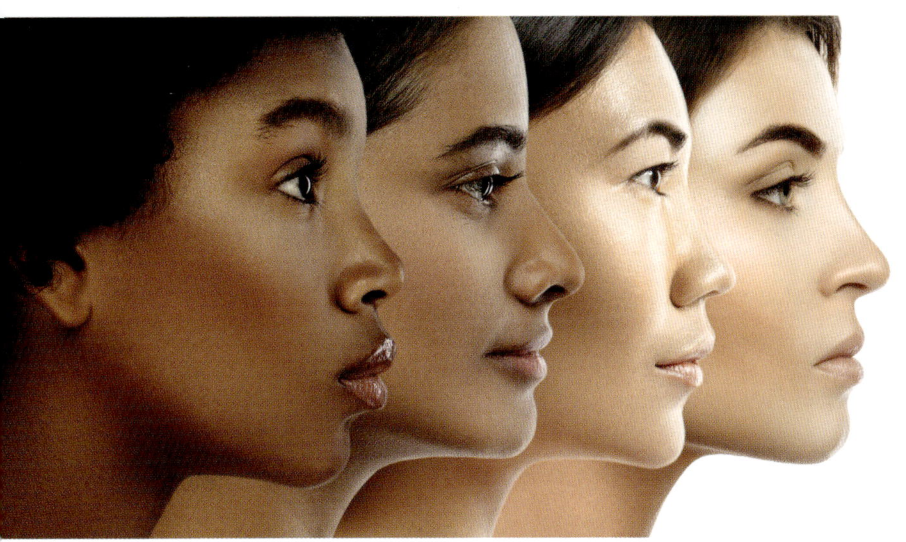

Undertone is a major element in the cosmetics industry. Skin ranges in undertone between a CIELAB hue angle of about twenty-two degrees to about sixty-eight degrees. The undertone is more apparent when shown against a white background.

98 UNIQUE HUES

Colors considered to be perceptually pure without any evidence of other hues

- Ewald Hering first defined the unique hues (also known as psychological color primaries) as red, green, yellow, and blue, observing that these four colors cannot be simultaneously perceived. Other colors always appear as combinations of these hues. For example, orange can be perceived as a mixture of red and yellow.

- Hering's system is based on two sets of opposite or opponent colors: red/green and yellow/blue. These, along with a white/black pair, form the basis of the Natural Color System.

- Although physiological opponency is clearly a mechanism that contributes to the phenomenon of unique hues, the actual opponent colors in the visual system are not the same as the unique hues.

Although unique blue, yellow, and green exist in the spectrum, there is no unique red. All the reds in the spectrum are too yellowish to be considered unique. Unique red is a nonspectral color.

SEE ALSO Natural Color System • Three Dimensions of Color

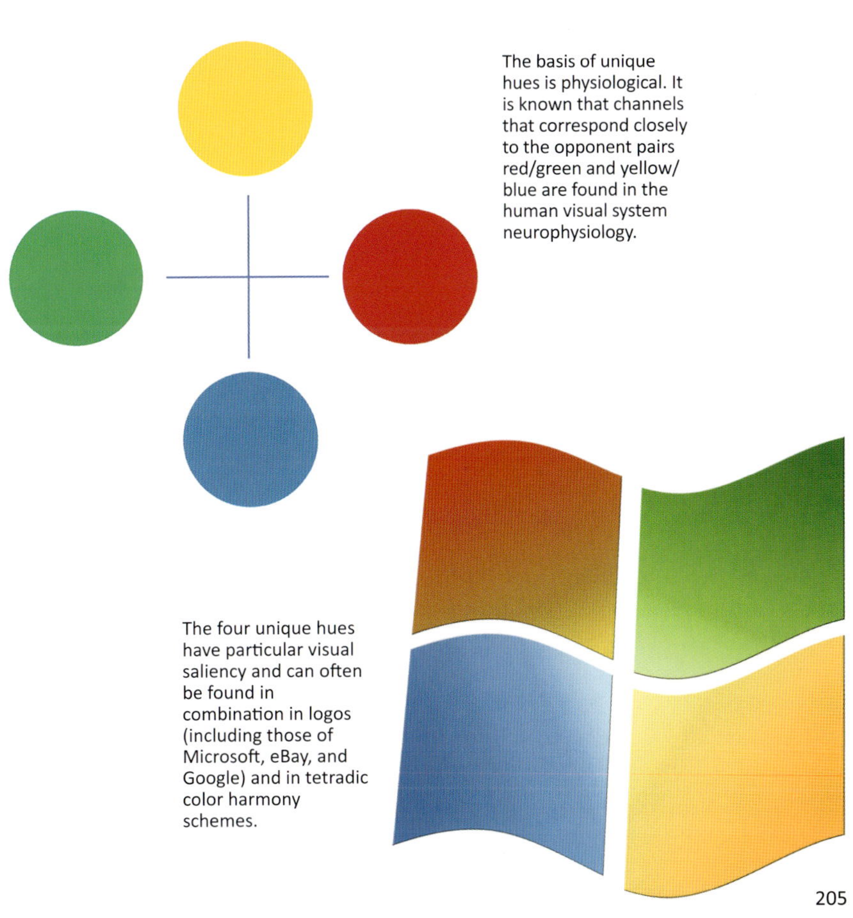

The basis of unique hues is physiological. It is known that channels that correspond closely to the opponent pairs red/green and yellow/blue are found in the human visual system neurophysiology.

The four unique hues have particular visual saliency and can often be found in combination in logos (including those of Microsoft, eBay, and Google) and in tetradic color harmony schemes.

99 WARM AND COOL

The colors of objects and lights can appear warm or cool mainly depending on their hue

- In 1813 Charles Hayter produced the first hue wheel that represented half the hues as warm and the other half as cool. Reds, yellows, and oranges were warm, whereas blues and greens were cool.

- In some art and design fields, warmer and cooler are used to discuss the relationship between the colors of objects. In interior design, the terminology can describe the psychological feeling of a space, especially with respect to the quality of the lighting. Light at a low color temperature is considered warmer than light at a higher color temperature.

- There is no consensus for describing a blue leaning toward red as either warm or cool. The same is true of orange. A shift in which direction—toward red or yellow—would be a cooler orange?

For clarity in communication, it is better to describe a shift in hue by naming the hue it moved toward, rather than using the terms warm *or* cool.

SEE ALSO Color Temperature

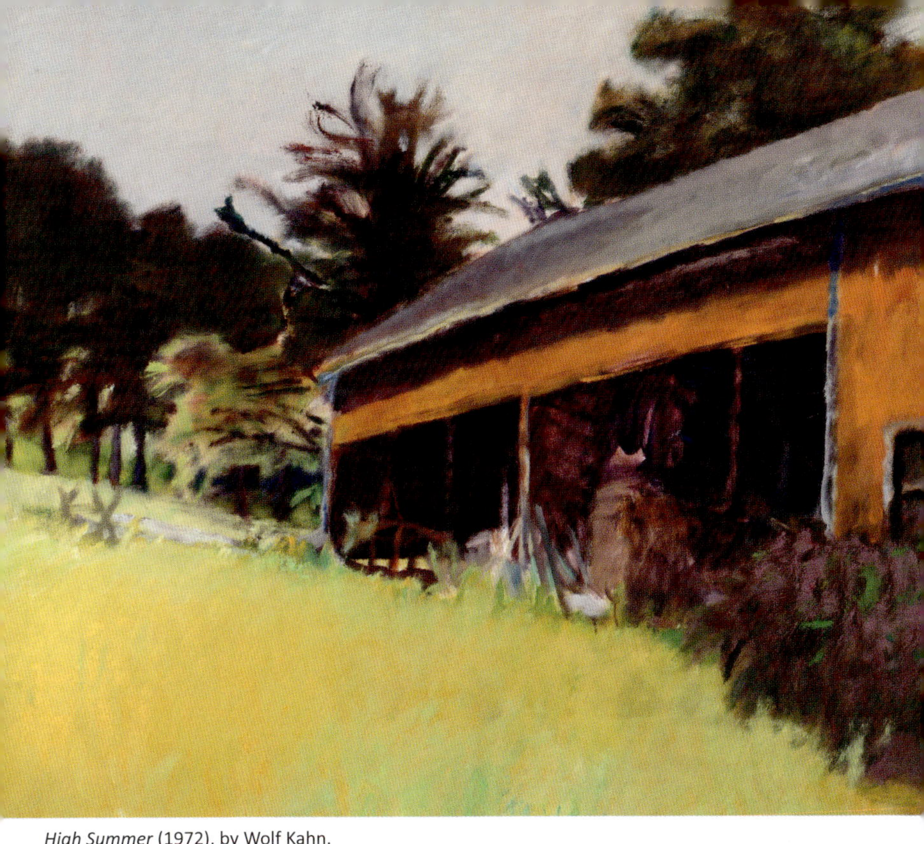

High Summer (1972), by Wolf Kahn.

100 WHITE BALANCE

The setting that ensures color fidelity in an image by establishing a baseline for the color of white in cameras and monitors

- The goal of performing a white balance is to render neutral colors (such as white and gray) appropriately, usually according to a specified color temperature.

- White balance is a feature of high-end digital camera systems and can typically be set either manually or automated. In the case of automatic white balance, the camera software will use algorithms that are inspired by an understanding of the human process of color constancy. Often such automatic algorithms try to ascertain the color temperature of the ambient illumination.

- For emissive displays, the white balance can usually be adjusted using settings on the display. White balance is an important feature in most color management pipelines that ensure color fidelity when color images are transmitted between different imaging devices. The unknown state of the white balance of many consumer displays is a challenge for retailers who are concerned with color fidelity on the internet.

SEE ALSO Color Management

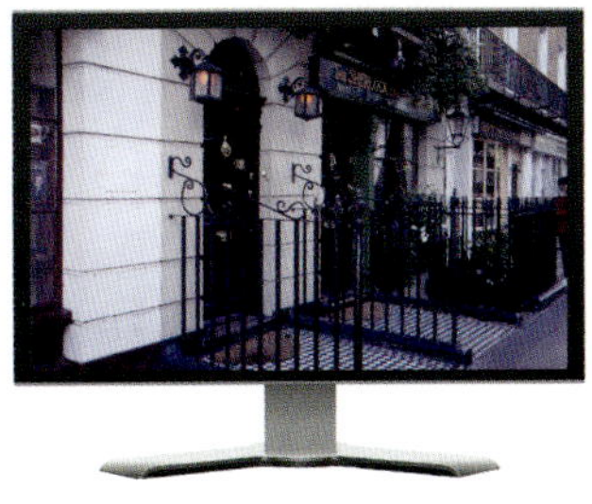

The same image is displayed on three emissive displays, which have different white points. The display on the left is set to a lower color temperature, and the display on the right is set to a higher color temperature, relative to the middle display.

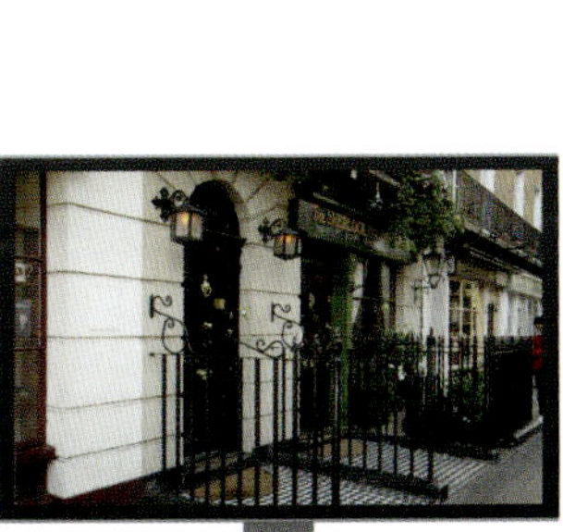

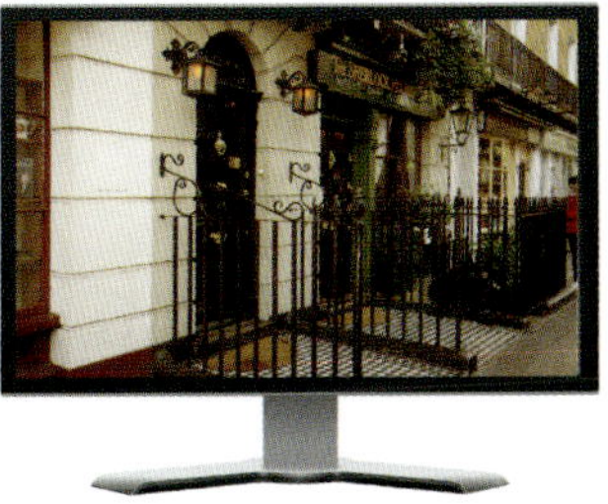

Acknowledgments

At Rockport Publishers, we must thank many people, especially Joy Aquilino for suggesting we coauthor this book, Jonathan Simcosky and John Gettings for keeping us on track, and David Martinell for his immense help during the layout process. A book on color would not be complete without images to accompany the text, so we need to give a huge thank-you to the many designers, artists, architects, and photographers who gave us permission to include their work in the book. A special thank-you to the members of the Joint ISCC/AIC Colour Literacy Project team for their contributions to the book and to Robert Hirschler, Luanne Stovall, and Karen Triedman who reviewed drafts and provided critical feedback.

Maggie Maggio and Stephen Westland

I would like to thank all my students over the years who asked questions I could not answer. Their curiosity inspired my deep dive into the universe of color. I would like to thank Stephen Westland for inviting me to coauthor this book. I am grateful for his wide-ranging expertise on the complex subject of color, his dedication to dispelling misconceptions, and his commitment to expanding our understanding of color to meet the evolving needs of the twenty-first century. Working together over the past two years has been a pleasure. Finally, I must thank my husband, Chuck Maggio, for his support and patience during the times when the deadlines loomed large and all my attention was focused on this book. **—MM**

I would like to thank Maggie Maggio for making the hard work and long hours that went into putting this book together enjoyable and rewarding. Without Maggie I could never have written this book. I would also like to thank all of my students over the many years from whom I have learned so much; it is, with them in mind, that I have written this book. Finally, I must thank Jane and Tyler for their endless patience during the many evenings when I needed to engage with Zoom calls. **—SW**

About the Authors

Maggie Maggio is a designer, artist, and art educator who has studied, taught, and worked with color for over forty years. Her personal explorations into the science of light and pigments led to the creation of workshops for artists and designers who want to incorporate the latest research in color science into their creative practice. As a member of the board of directors of the US Inter-Society Color Council (ISCC) and co-chair of the International Color Association Study Group on Color Education, Maggie focuses on bridging between the art, science, and industry of color and advancing color literacy for the twenty-first century. She is the current chair of the Joint International Color Association/ISCC Color Literacy Project, advocating for the integration of art and science in color education programs worldwide.

Stephen Westland is Professor of Color Science and Technology in the School of Design at the University of Leeds (UK). He was previously head of the School of Design at Leeds (2006–2013). His research interests are color design, color vision, and color measurement, and he has published over 250 peer-reviewed papers, book chapters, and books about these topics. He is a fellow of the Society of Dyers and Colourists and was president of the Society in 2019. In 2008 he was awarded the Davies Medal from the Royal Photographic Society (London) for his color research. He has won numerous research grants from both government and industry and has recently worked with AkzoNobel, Colgate, and Unilever on color-related projects. He holds several visiting professorships including at the University of Texas (U.S.) and Huazhong University of Science and Technology in Wuhan (China).

Photo Credits

11: (l) Courtesy of Dr. Anya Hurlbert, (r) Westland/Maggio; 13: Westland/Maggio; 15: (t) Zátonyi Sándor, (ifj.) Fizped/Wikimedia Commons (WC), (r) Nuria Estape; 17: Westland/Maggio; 19: Album/Alamy Stock Photo; 23: Dennis Jarvis/WC; 24: Munsell/Cleland; 25: Westland/Maggio; 27: Tegula/Pixabay; 29: Westland/Maggio; 31: National Archives and Records Administration, Records of the National Park Service/WC; 33: Pixabay; 35: Squirrel photos/Pixabay; 37: Nedd3_89/Pixabay; 39: Westland/Maggio; 41: Westland/Maggio; 43: Galleria Nazionale d'Arte Antica/WC; 45: Westland/Maggio; 47: geralt/Pixabay; 49: Holger Everding/WC; 51: geralt/Pixabay; 53: (l) Westland/Maggio, (r) Nicoline Kinch; 55: Harald Arnkil; 57: agefotostock/Alamy Stock Photo; 59: Cars Down Under/Flickr; 61: Westland/Maggio; 63: Ad Oculos/Shutterstock; 65: Ellen Divers; 66: Westland/Maggio; 67: Westland/Maggio; 69: Westland/Maggio; 71: (b) Westland/Maggio; 73: Westland/Maggio; 75: Westland/Maggio; 77: Neale Cousland/Shutterstock; 79: Collage Kaffe; 81: Westland/Maggio; 83: Silvestri Matteo; 85: Ken Howard/Alamy Stock Photo; 87: Westland/Maggio; 89: Orlagh O'Brien; 91: Hella Jongerius; 93: Library of Congress original/WC; 95: f11photo/Shutterstock; 97: James Gurney; 99: (t) Bischoff49/Pixabay, (b) Dezalb/Pixabay; 101: Westland/Maggio; 103: JuliaBoldt/Pixabay; 106: Dieric Bouts/WC; 107: Heidelberg University Library; 109: Westland/Maggio; 111: David Briggs; 113: Westland/Maggio; 115: Heritage Image Partnership Ltd/Alamy Stock Photo; 117: Nick Sherman/Flickr; 119: Luís Ribes Mateu; 123: Westland/Maggio; 123: alexandre zveiger/Shutterstock; 125: Stanislav Duben/Shutterstock; 127: David Briggs; 129: Bru-nO/Pixabay; 131: Westland/Maggio; 135: Renzo Shamey; 139: Westland/Maggio; 145: leemelina08/Pixabay; 147: stux/Pixabay; 149: Roy Osborne; 151: (t) Followtheflow/Shutterstock, (b) World History Archive/Alamy Stock Photo; 153: Westland/Maggio; 155: Westland/Maggio; 157: Moritz Zwimpfer; 159: ParentRap/Pixabay; 161: Robert Hirschler; 163: David Briggs; 165: EGL21/Pixabay; 167: Francesco Rugi; 169: (l)Tanya Paquet; 171: (b) Westland/Maggio; 173: Westland/Maggio; 177: (t) Mila Drumeva/Shutterstock; (b) udaix/Shutterstock; 177: PeterKraayvanger/Pixabay; 179: Spencer Finch; 181: Westland/Maggio; 183: Esa Naukkarinen; 185: Uri Rosenheck/WC; 189: (t) Tom McKinnon/Flickr (b) Prawny/Pixabay; 191: (l) Dan Adams, (r) Cynthia Toops; 193: Westland/Maggio; 195: Jacobolus/WC; 197: rawpixel; 199: Michael James; 201: Concetta Antico; 203: BLACKDAY/Shutterstock; 205: Westland/Maggio; 207: Gift of the Sara Roby Foundation; 209: Westland/Maggio